DIRTY LITTLE SECRETS OF BUZZ

How to Attract Massive Attention
for Your Business, Your Product, or Yourself

DAVID SEAMAN

SOURCEBOOKS, INC.
NAPERVILLE, ILLINOIS

Published by Sourcebooks, Inc.
P.O. Box 4410, Naperville, Illinois 60567–4410
(630) 961–3900
Fax: (630) 961–2168
www.sourcebooks.com

Library of Congress Cataloging-in-Publication Data

Seaman, David.
  Dirty little secrets of buzz : how to attract massive attention for your business, your product, or yourself / by David Seaman.
    p. cm.
  1. Publicity. 2. Industrial publicity. 3. Marketing. I. Title.
  HD59.S43 2008
  659.2—dc22
                                    2008014860

Printed and bound in the United States of America.
VP 10 9 8 7 6 5 4 3 2 1

Acknowledgments

Emmanuelle Alspaugh, my agent at Wendy Sherman Associates.

At Sourcebooks: Shana Drehs, Erin Nevius (who has hawk-like editing abilities), and Sara Kase. In the publicity department, Liz Kelsch and Heather Moore.

My family, friends, newsletter subscribers, and—of course—all of the media professionals consulted for this book. Thank you!

Contents

Preface:

★
★
★ ★
★

· ·

★

Consider Yourself Warned

Author's warning: *Dirty Little Secrets of Buzz* is written in a somewhat amoral tone: I'm giving you the tools without preaching to you. I do strongly advise you to use these fast buzz secrets for good—either to improve your circumstances or to benefit those around you. These secrets work, and often swiftly, so be prepared for the consequences. **Once you become famous, there is no guarantee of ever returning to obscurity. Your actions will no longer be your own.**

Here are just some of the secrets you'll find inside:

- Create real outrage
- Michael Moore's secret of continued success
- Establish a positive connection with the public
- Change is absolutely necessary
- Always remain accessible to the media
- Feel like you deserve to be on the air
- Think like a successful television producer
- Have an enemy and publicize your rivalry
- Everyone looks and sounds better on-air
- Build loyalty at any cost, even if it means less privacy

- Keep your fans involved and intrigued
- Exploit the viral aspects of YouTube and Vimeo
- Send Facebook video messages to your core fans only
- Create a viral group on Facebook
- Take advantage of slow news days
- Test new marketing concepts online first
- Network with others in your field
- Appear in-demand at all times
- Make everything appear easier than it actually is
- Be flexible and willing to evolve with the news cycle
- Take advantage of personal relationships, online and offline
- Befriend the print media, especially trade magazines
- Parlay one television appearance into many
- Turn your website into a repeat publicity trap
- Be seen as a controversial expert, not an average Joe
- Use public appearances as a way to recruit new fans
- Don't ride a publicity wave past its peak
- Get invited back on radio shows
- Remain down-to-earth, or at least fake humility
- Make the show's host your ally
- Anticipate the newest stories before others do

Introduction:

Welcome to the Media Feeding Frenzy

FAME IS LIKE A RIVER, THAT BEARETH UP THINGS LIGHT AND SWOLLEN, AND DROWNS THINGS WEIGHTY AND SOLID.

—*Francis Bacon, 1561–1626*

The burst of camera flashes and the chaos of having a swarm of television crews around you is exhilarating—and more than a little weird.

"You'll be all over the world tomorrow," a well-connected tabloid photographer quietly tells me.

"Cool!" I respond. A microphone is shoved in my direction. It has the red *TV Guide* logo on it, and I'm asked a bunch of questions. I respond easily enough, although I'm somewhat dehydrated. I don't think I've had a chance to stop and drink water for the past four hours.

A few minutes later, a CNN camera crew wants to interview me. I agree. As I begin to answer their questions, my phone vibrates. I answer and am informed I'm now live on a major CBS Radio show out of Los Angeles. I tell the guy who's speaking, "Let me call you back in five minutes. I'm in the middle of something."

He flat-out refuses. "You're on the air," he reminds me.

So I talk about the chaos around me for a few minutes—try to bring this all into perspective for those listening in their cars and their cubicles in L.A. *This* being a faux protest composed of three people, one of whom is a professional Paris Hilton imitator, and a literal swarm of national media. We're on an otherwise neglected sidewalk in SoHo, there to protest the jailing of Paris Hilton and demand her release after she was jailed for violating her probation in June 2007. If it weren't for the reporters tapping on their BlackBerrys and the *cl-cl-cl* of camera shutters, it would be nearly silent.

I should add that I actually believed Paris was being singled out because of her public image; I wasn't being disingenuous. It was a "faux" protest because there were only three of us, and because each of us obviously understood this wasn't really the most important issue out there.

"You should chant 'Free Paris!'" a producer suggests. I think this is a killer idea (will look great on the clips), so we start to yell "FREE PARIS, FREE PARIS" with less than total enthusiasm. We start to laugh, and some of the press laugh with us. This is ridiculous.

And that's the story of how I came to field test the powerful secrets of buzz—the strategies that can create a national sensation out of essentially nothing. Just imagine how these techniques will work for you once we come up with a coherent media message together.

In this book I'm going to share with you the secrets of attracting massive media attention. These are the black arts, the skills and loopholes you won't learn in any college marketing course.

I don't care why you want the attention. Maybe you have a worthy cause you want to raise awareness for; perhaps there is some hot new injustice the world *needs* to know about. Maybe you're just a publicity whore or creative type lusting for global celebrity. If that's you, feel no shame. Artists and musicians need a certain level of buzz savvy to get their art the attention it deserves. At a certain point, what you create will speak for itself. But for right now, you need to tell the world. This is a critical moment. Talent needs an audience. If you own a small business or are responsible for marketing a product, you need buzz as well—it's more cost-effective than traditional advertising (buzz is often completely free) and can jump-start sales in a jaw-dropping way.

I'll show you how to spark a media feeding frenzy. What better way to get your art (or yourself) in front of millions? In the case of the Free Paris campaign, I created a web page in approximately twenty minutes. I told the right outlets about it, with precisely the right hook, and three days later I was interviewed by Nancy Grace on CNN. The site was featured on MSNBC.

Things took off very quickly at that point. I was invited back on CNN. A German TV network showed up at my apartment, hoping to get an exclusive. I appeared in numerous celebrity tabloid weeklies, including *In Touch* and *Life & Style*. The campaign was written about in nearly all of the New York dailies, including the *Post,* the *Sun, News-day, AM New York, Metro,* and so on. I was lightheartedly ripped on ABC's *Jimmy Kimmel Live*, and Conan O'Brien mentioned the protest in his monologue.

Then, having made my point and gotten my fifteen minutes of fame, I virtually disappeared; sometimes it's crucial to appear less than eager; news producers love a challenge. I turned down subsequent TV interviews and gutted the web page. Now it is little more than a list of links to various outlets where the story ran, and plugs for two causes actually worth covering.

It didn't *have* to be Paris; it just so happened it was her. My technique works for any hot news item. If the media is talking about it, you can learn how to become a part of that discussion. Getting publicity boils down to just a set of skills and nothing more. Attracting media coverage becomes easy, even routine, with practice.

The Free Paris campaign wasn't my first success. I created a storm of publicity surrounding the release of my first book (*The Real Meaning of Life*, New World Library, 2005) and then stepped back from it all, so it would appear to be entirely "spontaneous." People love to hear that your success is somehow an accident, that you've done nothing at all to spark the media's interest. You'll learn to play into this.

My main point is this: **I don't play by traditional rules, and neither should you**. The old rules tell you to play nice, to slowly work your way up the ladder, to build contacts over many years, to keep everything neat and tidy. Follow those rules only if you don't want to start a sensation. Otherwise, read on. You'll need to embrace chaos, and create it, if you want to get the national media's atten-

★ | **4**

tion. The book is broken into eleven chapters, each one containing valuable mass-media secrets and powerful tools. You will also find case studies and interviews with newsmakers. Sometimes the easiest way to adopt a new strategy is to see how others have benefited from it.

CHAPTER 1

Choose Your Own Adventure

SECRET #1: FAME AND GLORY:
For the Company or For Yourself?

"For England, James?" asks Bond's enemy in the film *GoldenEye*, moments before 007 finishes him off. "No, for me," Bond replies without an ounce of regret, allowing the villain to fall to his death.

First and foremost, you need to figure out if you are in search of buzz for yourself or for your company. While the techniques used will be strikingly similar, the outcome is often quite different. In the case of a small business owner, the ultimate goal is sales and massive new revenue streams—buzz accomplishes this by lowering your advertising costs. In fact, buzz is often free. In the case of an individual (such as an artist, actor, musician or author), buzz is designed to create greater opportunities and a larger market for your work. A successful buzz campaign will create a built-in audience of thousands, eager and ready to spread the word about you. Life-changing opportunity comes when people know about you. For the first time in history, the leap from "unknown" to "household name" can be accomplished virtually overnight. The mechanism for doing this, of course, is the Internet.

So if you are an individual in search of lasting fame, read the first scenario, "Comfortably Well Known ('Microfame')." If you are a business owner or marketing executive, read the second scenario, "Business Firing on All Buzz Cylinders."

★ Scenario #1: Comfortably Well Known ("Microfame")

You wake up in the morning and before showering, log in to MySpace, where you briefly survey your online empire (58,000 friends and growing). You respond to a few messages and then check your email: among the random, eccentric messages from fans are an interview request and a query from a TV production company interested in developing an online series with you.

The vast majority of your MySpace friends, along with your contacts on rival networking site Facebook (more on these two bastions of buzz in Chapter Four), check your blog regularly for updates. Oh, and of course you have a blog, and it's a combination of simple-text entries and enthusiastic, pithy YouTube video posts. The site's traffic isn't unbelievable, but it's growing at around 20 percent a month, and your following is a fiercely loyal one. The blog makes $500 a weekday and slightly more on weekends, thanks to text ads from Google AdSense that you have strategically placed toward the top of the blog ("above the fold" in advertising lingo). This revenue lets you know you're on the right track, and if it keeps up, you plan on hiring a full-time assistant next month to help with some of the blog posts and video editing.

You've just finished reading a hilarious new book—maybe something by Augusten Burroughs or David Sedaris—and you want to share it with your fans. You post a quick review to your blog (this takes around fifteen minutes) and provide an Amazon Associates link to the book. This way, you'll earn a commission from Amazon on every copy sold through your site's recommendation link. You check back the next day, and while it isn't a windfall, 152 fans have decided to take you up on your recommendation. That's around $170 in commission for fifteen minutes of work. And you *know* your readers will love the book. When you recommend something of serious value, your blog's readers trust you even more.

While you aren't "famous" in the same way that, say, Oprah Winfrey or Jude Law or Lindsay Lohan are famous, you are aware that what you're doing is not entirely normal. You are getting paid essentially for having opinions and sharing those opinions. And, beyond the great pay and conspicuous lack of a boss, you are vaguely aware that you have an impact on the world. While millions of others simply consume mass media and occasionally grumble about how the latest installment in the *Pirates of the Caribbean* franchise didn't quite live up to the hype, you are interacting with media. Without trying, you've become a powerful gatekeeper who helps thousands of readers determine what's worth checking out.

Despite the sophistication of search engines, people still want a real person they can trust and agree with on most issues. Over the next six months, people who have discovered your site and like you will tell their friends to check you out. Your site's growth is now *astounding* (but entirely predictable), and by early next year you'll have one million readers per month. Welcome to microfame! At this point, it becomes relatively easy to branch out into whatever creative outlet suits you best—writing, pursuing that music career you've had on the back burner, even taking a stab at television work.

A year ago, indie music labels and mid-size publishers would have laughed in your face if you sent them an unsolicited proposal or demo album. Now things are a little different: No one is laughing at your million readers per month. Publishers realize that if only 5 percent of your fans end up buying a book written by you, that's fifty thousand copies sold—extremely strong sales for a first-time author. Independent music labels realize that your following is large enough to get a debut album off the ground or at least give it a good shot of selling well. It's worth the risk to them, which means you're already in the door.

★ **Scenario #2: Business Firing on All Buzz Cylinders**
The quote from Henry John Heinz on the back of Heinz brand ketchup should be the credo of every entrepreneur in America: "To do a common thing uncommonly well brings success." You don't need to come up with a whole new niche. In fact, being the first in a new niche is dangerous because you don't know how large the actual market is for your product or service. You spend time and money developing the need, and then someone savvier swoops in and benefits from your trailblazing. It's far easier to do something that people already understand (celebrity gossip, air travel, hotels—hell, even ketchup) and execute it better than anyone else in the industry. Consumers often judge a product by its reputation and buzz. Have

others heard of it? Do others use it? Is it a hot item or is it out of fashion?

I'm assuming you already have a product that kicks ass. Hyperbole can only go so far; at a certain point, you need a killer product to back it up. Apple, although far from an upstart at this point, is the perfect example of this. The company spends massive time and energy on its buzz effort. This gets early adopters to buy—the company sold 270,000 iPhones within the first thirty hours of the product's launch. By the end of 2008, many are expecting Apple to have sold ten million iPhone units. A lot of these customers, including your humble author, were influenced to action by recommendations from friends and non-traditional buzz.

Unfortunately, I cannot help you create a killer product or service. But I can help you get attention for it— the kind of attention that convinces early adopters to buy your product.

Here is the ideal, and what this book will show you how to do: Within days of your product's launch, mentions in key media venues spark early interest and provoke controversy. People are now curious about your company, your product, and what you might do next. Simultaneously, blogs are busy publishing unofficial reports on your product, complete with early reviews and raving testimonials. Google, Microsoft Live, Yahoo! Search, and the other key English-language search engines are sending a flood of targeted visitors to your simple text-based site. Even at three o'clock in the morning, thousands of search engine users are finding your product for the first time. Those who don't initially buy your product from your site will seek out information and reviews. And you'll "catch" these potential buyers, taking their email addresses and other key points of contact. If you don't make the sale today, you'll make it tomorrow or the day after. More important than the sale is credibility. You will become an expert and a source of authority within the marketplace where your product can be found. Trust, combined with bursts of massive media attention, leads to sales and the first bridge of loyalty between customer and company.

Due to the social nature of Internet gossip and the susceptibility of mainstream media to such chatter, your product's profile will grow quickly—and without any expense on your part. When your company reaches the point where it makes sense to purchase targeted online advertising, you'll know exactly where to buy and why. And you'll know how to maximize (and monetize) each click. Buzz can help small businesses go from "unknown" to "household name" just as easily as it can help people do so—it all depends on how you use it.

SECRET #2: BE OUTRAGEOUS OR DIE!

Another common theme explored in this book is the powerful hunger for uniqueness—and the odd benefits of outrage. Yes, I said benefits: It's often better to piss someone off than to leave them entirely ambivalent. Regardless of whether you're promoting yourself or a product, outrageous behavior will help get you attention.

Let's say you watch a movie at the local multiplex with your friends on a Friday night. The film is so-so: If you were forced to rate it, you'd give it a six out of ten. (Let's also say, hypothetically, that Nicolas Cage is the lead.) On the surface, this sounds all right. However, from a buzz perspective, it's potentially worse than a score of one out of ten. If you throw something out into the world and you want it to be universally loved—whether it be a press release, a new short video on YouTube, or a media product of any kind—it needs to truly kick ass. It needs to be *at least* a nine out of ten. People don't run out and tell their friends to see mediocre movies; they don't forward links to semi-amusing YouTube videos; they don't vote for political candidates running on the "meh, why not?" platform. And if you don't have the savvy to create real enthusiasm, snag that truly awful review. Why? Because it will create curiosity and spur controversy.

Look at the hailstorm of publicity stirred up by Mel Gibson's *Passion of the Christ.* Say what you will about the film's merits (or lack thereof). The fact of the matter is that he managed to get millions of dollars in free advertising— the cable news networks chattered about it relentlessly and the blogs were ablaze with comments from moviegoers. I saw it for the sole reason that I wanted to form an opinion on it. Had it not been for the massive controversy, I can assure you I would not have seen it.

Let's be straight here: Buzz is not the only way to create action. You can also blanket a city with expensive bill-boards, take out a multimillion-dollar TV campaign, or work with an established Hollywood publicist. These will all create serious attention. But buzz can create just as much of a stir without spending any money at all and without having any initial media connections (you'll build them as you go along).

The core ingredients of buzz are easy to grasp: Outrage and great content. People want a killer story they can gossip about with coworkers the next day and get different, passionate opinions; television producers want to be the ones who presented this story to these viewers; and blog editors want the credit for creating the early interest and getting the TV producers interested. This is obviously a huge oversimplification of the buzz ecosystem, and it doesn't always work this way, but you can see the rough outline of the process. You can also see how buzz benefits everyone involved—the person it concerns, the blogs that launch it, and the television shows that capitalize on it.

The story has to be great, meaning it has to be different from all of the noise out there. There's more competition than ever before for media coverage. The potential payoff is also greater than ever. If you can't stand out from the other stories and the millions of wannabes posting cat videos to YouTube, where does that leave you?

Outrage is the key. Although it's now old news, *Fahrenheit 9/11* was not a timid film. Michael Moore wanted to create an incendiary must-see—and it paid off in a big way, becoming the highest-grossing documentary film of all time.

15 ★

I'm not saying that you need to intentionally upset people. It's enough to have an outrageous personality, or to say something on national television (or even just on your blog) that everyone else is *thinking* but not saying. These are how talk-show personalities like Bill Maher get ahead. This is how anonymous bloggers become online superstars and eventually cross over into the mainstream.

This is also how great products become great—without spending a dime. I don't know about you, but for a while I was hearing a lot of crazy stories about the popular energy drink Red Bull. Among the most disturbing, several people told me that some kid in Europe *died* from a Red Bull "overdose." I bet you've heard a variation of that story. Now, is this a bogus urban legend? Of course it is. But it gets people talking about their brand of energy drink. Word of mouth is one of the most powerful forms of free buzz. What other soft drink benefits from such word of mouth? When was the last time a friend ran up to you and excitedly said, "Dude, I've got a funny story about Coca-Cola"? For more on the insane tale of Red Bull's word-of-mouth campaigns, go out and immediately buy *Brand Hijack* by Alex Wipperfurth. It's a brilliant book, and I would be lying if I told you it hasn't influenced my views on buzz marketing.

Enough about outrage for now. You'll get a better feel for this once you master the rules of effective publicity whoring. Read on.

ANN COULTER: CRAZY SELLS

If you say outrageous things often enough and you have decent contacts, you will get blog mentions, invitations to radio shows, and TV bookings. Quite possibly a lot of them. But you need to make sure you're saying things that are at least relatively coherent. If you just randomly spew hatred and unsubstantiated opinion, you aren't an expert at buzz building. You're a televised circus freak.

I *do* encourage you to be outrageous, because that's what ultimately attracts viewers—and therefore, that's what makes you valuable to shows as a repeat guest. But be outrageous in a way that makes sense. Go after the powers that be in a fresh and original way.

I think it's possible to be outrageous and still have moral grounding. Without this, people may talk *about* you, but they won't trust you. And this lack of trust means that nobody really cares about what you have to say. This is the difference between Ann Coulter and someone like Bill Maher. Both of them say shocking things; both of them get a tremendous amount of media attention. But if you look at Maher's comments over the years, they are consistent. They make sense—and they promote certain clearly defined agendas (he hates hypocrisy, conservatives, and the fact that weed is still illegal). Ann Coulter's comments, in aggregate, don't really make sense: She hates whatever will get people talking about her.

17 | ★

CHAPTER 2

The Rules of Effective
Publicity Whoring

There are a lot of rules we have to follow in life—but as this isn't a self-help book, I'm not going to pretend to know all of them. However, I do know the rules of effective publicity whoring. Get them tattooed on the back of your hand, or, at the very least, get to know them as well as the back of your hand. I share them below, along with some valuable other starting tips. This chapter also serves as a taste of things to come, touching on many of the topics (search engine positioning, viral video success, managing unfavorable press) that will be addressed in greater detail a bit later.

SECRET #3: THE FIVE RULES

★ 1. Don't be boring!

The commercial, mainstream media work to make a profit. If people don't watch their stories, buy their papers, or click on their websites, they don't make a profit. For this reason, the media do have a structural bias. The moment something is resolved, it is no longer a story. Anna Nicole Smith became a media obsession because absolutely no areas of her life were resolved! Everything was controversy, intrigue, and chaos. Britney Spears remains controversial—and in the limelight—because her life has become synonymous with the phrase "train wreck." If she led a quiet life in the suburbs, the media attention surrounding her would fizzle out. While you're busy "sympathizing" with her (or not!), she is getting *millions* of dollars in free publicity from the outlets covering her every move. This non-stop buzz creates interest in her performances and any future albums.

Of course, since **credibility** is an important component, you probably want to find a way to excite without embarrassing yourself. The possibilities are endless, and this book gives you some ideas, but the *best* ideas will ultimately come from you. You know yourself, your style, and the product you're selling better than anyone else. Only you can find the perfect-fitting controversy. The key is action. Just like a good movie or entertaining book, buzz needs to have action and a "plot" to move things forward. A female blogger who supports libertarian presidential candidate Ron Paul? Not so exciting! But a female blogger who runs a site called *Strippers for Ron Paul?* Absolute genius (and, in case you're wondering, she gets plenty of press).

21 ★

Action can be online, in the form of a petition, or real— a protest in the streets, a war of words between two rival organizations, even just a well-publicized argument at a night club. These are the things that get media coverage, because these are the stories people tune in to hear. Only idiots send out boring press releases. Actually, allow me to correct that statement: Idiots send *only* press releases. Nobody cares about your product unless it can be woven into a compelling story.

Here's a perfect example of this: Video-game-system releases. When the new whatever comes out each year, as it inevitably does (a new Xbox or PlayStation or Nintendo system), the media devotes a lot of attention to it. They know there are a ton of video-game addicts out there who will sit up and pay attention. Of course, the media can't simply plug the systems. That's boring and will turn away the millions of people (like me) who don't really care about video games. Instead, they report from the "front lines" with unbelievable stories of parents fighting each other for PlayStation 3 and unkempt nerds waiting in line for *days* for Nintendo Wii. This way, everyone wins: Gamers hear about the much-anticipated new gaming platforms, and gainfully employed people get to shake their heads and mutter about how ridiculous life has become.

If you get only one thing out of this book, other than a finely crafted paperweight, it should be this: **Controversy is good.** The mainstream media is not, for the most part, an infomercial network. It wants interesting stories and doesn't care about plugging you or your company. That will be a helpful side effect, but rarely is it a reporter's primary intention to make you richer. As another example of controversy, look at movie reviews. If a movie gets "all right" reviews from all the major sources, I may or may not see it. If it gets one or a few *amazing* reviews, and then some really negative reviews, I am actually much more likely to see it. Why is this? Because my curiosity is piqued. If one critic says, "Go see *Sweeney Todd;* Johnny Depp is great in it," and another says, "It's too bloody and violent," my curiosity is suddenly piqued: *How* bloody? *How* violent? Great buzz actually asks more questions than it answers. An iPhone TV commercial doesn't browbeat you with a list of every useful feature. Instead, it piques your curiosity and lets you make the next move.

British graffiti artist Banksy has become something of a favorite among the Hollywood elite, garnering interest from A-listers such as Brad Pitt and receiving more than his fair share of media coverage. Why? Because he is controversial and most people don't know his identity. The graffiti has an overtly political message—at times apparently anti-globalization, at other times mocking the British police. Of course, graffiti is entirely illegal in the first place. It's risky, his identity is cloaked in mystery, and the finished works of art are *cool* looking. This is the perfect recipe for buzz. Great back story and a buzzworthy product.

★ 2. Build on an existing story.

Unless your name has "President" in front of it or you're already an established star in some medium, chances are pretty good the media won't let you create stories from scratch. You might be able to if there were an absolutely amazing hook or an especially brilliant idea, but it wouldn't be easy—and I'm all about keeping things easy. Find an existing story, something that people care about and the media has its beady eyes on, and then find a unique angle. Find your way into hot stories that already exist.

Look at Chris Crocker, the "Leave Britney Alone!" guy. Chances are, if you know who I'm talking about, you just rolled your eyes dismissively or in actual disgust. That's good: If you are not rabidly in support of something or actively disgusted by it, then it has no viral potential. "Viral" means that a video or other piece of online content is swiftly spread by others through word of mouth, usually as a link sent in email, posted to message boards, and "up-voted" on social bookmarking sites such as Del.icio.us (we'll get to these in Chapter 3: All Fires Start with a Spark).

If you don't know who Crocker is, he's a guy who posted a screechy YouTube video in defense of Britney Spears—the video was timed perfectly, released after her meltdown at the MTV Video Music Awards. A guy posting a YouTube tirade is nothing new; a guy so adamantly offended by something absurd *is* new. The video enjoyed massive viral spread and hoisted Crocker into the hallowed halls of Internet fame. In other words, he built on an existing story.

Sometimes, you don't *want* to be a wholly original story. Look at what happened to confused "U.S. American" Miss Teen South Carolina. She was asked on national television at the Miss Teen USA pageant why a fifth of Americans could not identify their own country on a map. Her response, verbatim, was as follows: "I personally believe the U.S. Americans are unable to do so because, uh, some, uh . . . people out there in our nation don't have maps, and, uh, I believe that our education like such as South Africa and, uh, the Iraq everywhere like, such as and . . . I believe that they should, our education over here in the U.S. should help the U.S., err, uh, should help South Africa and should help the Iraq and the Asian countries, so we will be able to build up our future for our . . . "

Her incoherent ramble was viewed *millions of times* on YouTube and replayed on just about every single talk show.

Jimmy Kimmel remarked during his monologue that he personally must have watched the YouTube video about "three million times." Of course, even this embarrassing moment for Miss Teen South Carolina had its silver lining: Continued "relevance," greater recognition, and a softball appearance on the *Today* show in which host Matt Lauer commiserates with her ("We do live television every day… Caitlin, I can't even count the number of times I've said things and then we've all gone to commercial break and we've looked at each other like, 'What did you just say?'"). Lauer also contends in the segment that her YouTube fame is something of a "double-edged sword," which is really the perfect way to describe it. Even flat-out silly press is often better than no press whatsoever.

25 ★

★ 3. Let them find you.

You could spam a thousand television producers and get no response whatsoever. Or, you could build online word-of-mouth buzz and—within a matter of hours—have producers frantically calling you to schedule an interview. Create the buzz, and then make it easy for them to find you. This is, in reality, how it happens. You check your email, and there are interview requests from various shows. "Carpet-bombing" overworked producers around the country with your pitch is not likely to yield anything meaningful.

You also should work out your basic search-engine positioning several weeks *before* you stage any kind of serious media event. If you're talking about your wine store's upcoming event on a radio show, even if the host is gracious and mentions your site's URL and your store's address, few people are going to write that down. Most will be busy at work or in their cars. Many listeners will Google you later in the day: "San Diego wine-store tasting" or something similar. If your site doesn't immediately pop up within the first page of results, you have lost a potential lifetime customer. Or, if you've heard me rambling on the radio about this book, chances are you didn't write down the exact title and immediately head to your closest chain bookstore to purchase a copy. People don't act like sheep. Buzz is always far more dynamic and sometimes unpredictable. Instead, you may have done a search for "guy talking about dynamic fame," and my site popped up on the results page. That's smart marketing. We'll talk in detail later about exactly how to position a web page, but for now it's enough to know that you should include likely keywords on your site. Include phrases that visitors would likely use to find you after hearing you on the radio or seeing you on TV. Repeat them—on different areas of your website—at least three times so that the search engine "realizes" they are relevant terms and not just background noise. Include your name or your company's business name in the title of your web page so it is appropriately spidered (AKA indexed) by the search engine. This sounds like obvious stuff, but you would be *astounded* by the number of otherwise savvy companies who put "Homepage" or "Welcome" as the sole title tag for their website. This is an extraordinarily huge oversight: Nobody searching for you is going to find you if your title is something generic. It needs to be specific. There are ways to increase the odds of your site coming up on the first page of results, and we'll discuss them in Chapter 5.

★ 4. Know what you're getting into.

The media don't like or dislike *you*. They don't have any idea who you are as a person—how you treat your pets, what you're like in bed, whether you tip well. All that matters is the story. They either like it or they don't, or they know it will sell papers or it won't. You have to create a story they'll like and will sell.

Which of the following is more appealing as a hook: "Area Business Donates $1,000 to Charity" or "Local Bakery Gives $2 to Global Warming Fund for Every Customer Who Enters Store on Earth Day"? One story is bland, the other is intriguing. It's unusual, and you want to find out more about the bakery. Who owns it? A burnt-out hippie? A marketing genius? It raises questions and piques curiosity.

Everyone has seen the celebrity who starts to take things a little *too* personally, flicking off photographers and ranting about a lack of privacy. This may seem reasonable to the person doing these things, but to millions of casual observers it seems absolutely bat shit insane—and it creates instant resentment. After all, we see you flicking *us* off in the magazines, not the lanky photographer. If you don't like getting attention or reviews for your product (some of them potentially unfavorable), you shouldn't be in this game. There's an excellent quote by Fred Allen: "A celebrity is a person who works hard all his life to become known, then wears dark glasses to avoid being recognized."

★ 5. Short and sweet!

We have short attention spans in the twenty-first century. Your idea needs to be easily conveyed in a sentence or a quick burst of casual conversation. The other day I read about a guy who received a significant book deal for his idea: "Hot Chicks With Douchebags." I immediately thought, *That is brilliant.* As a dude living in New York, I can relate to the phenomenon of lame guys at nightclubs (the aforementioned douchebags) with unnaturally attractive women. The title conveys the entire premise of the guy's book, which is supposed to be a collection of photos! Whenever possible, find a cause that can be immediately conveyed in a title. Bonus points if it's intriguing enough to work its way into everyday conversation ("Did you see that Free Paris moron on CNN the other night?").

Even though the film ultimately had flaws and was met with less-than-stellar numbers at the box office, *Snakes on a Plane* had millions of bored people on the Internet absolutely enthralled based on only two pieces of advance information: (a) the transcendently amazing title and (b) Samuel L. Jackson's involvement.

***

Those are the rules. There's more to it than that, but those are the basics. We'll be working with those five throughout the book, so learn to love 'em! Before we get ahead of ourselves, let's take a look at some truly gifted publicity whores.

★ Sam Adams: Founding Father, Publicity Whore

Sam Adams (the patriot, not the ubiquitous beer brand!) was America's buzz pioneer. Adams regularly led town meetings, the blogosphere of his day, to generate interest in his various causes. During these meetings, he drafted written protests of various British taxes imposed upon the colonies.

Most famously, Adams was an architect of the Boston Tea Party—the ultimate publicity stunt. Eighty men dressed up as Mohawk Indians and boarded three tea ships at Boston Harbor. In about three hours, the faux Indians dumped all 342 chests of British tea overboard. Word of this spread like wildfire—it was just the right combination of crazy and rebellious to get colonial gossip-mongers chatting—and it led to the expedited opening of a Continental Congress.

★ The Naked Cowboy: The Absurd

Perhaps you've heard of Robert John Burck, better known to most New Yorkers as the Naked Cowboy. For the uninitiated, he is a man famous for strumming his guitar in Times Square while wearing only white underwear, boots, and a cowboy hat with the words "Naked Cowboy" emblazoned on the front of it.

Genius, right? Well, you be the judge, but in terms of media coverage, he is truly successful. He put a unique twist on street musicians, and his bizarre outfit appeals to chatty Midwestern tourists, who snap shots of him on their cell phone cameras and send them to friends at home.

Among numerous television appearances, the Naked Cowboy has parlayed his bizarre strand of fame into a lucrative career. He was part of USA Network's "Characters Welcome" campaign in 2006, had a cameo appearance in a Super Bowl commercial, and is reportedly recording his first album this year.

In addition to all that, he has his own brand of mobile ringtones, which can be downloaded for $1.99 each! As a recent TIME.com article by James Poniewozik sums it up, "Burck—inspired by the works of Tony Robbins—has parlayed a good bod, a decent voice, and the willingness to use them into a thriving merchandising-and-endorsements business."

★ Michael Moore: The Piggybacker

No introduction needs to be given for documentary filmmaker Michael Moore. The very name produces an immediate visceral reaction in almost every American—either a vigorous nodding of the head or an unrestrained cringe, depending on where you fall politically. But regardless of whether you agree with his social messages, there is a tremendous amount to be learned from his publicity technique.

Moore is a master practitioner of the Second Rule: Build on an existing story. His documentaries are responses to world events. *Roger & Me*, his 1989 film, was Moore's response to General Motors closing its factories in Flint, Michigan, and relocating to Mexico for the cheaper labor. It addressed our country's fears about outsourcing and losing American labor jobs to overseas competition.

Bowling for Columbine, his 2002 film, was a response to the Columbine school massacre. It tapped into our collective confusion and rage after that event occurred, and it went on to win the Academy Award for Documentary Feature that year.

Fahrenheit 9/11 was, of course, Moore's response to the 9/11 attacks and the Bush administration's handling of it. It tapped into our collective confusion and rage (sound familiar?) and generated so much controversy that it now holds the record for highest-grossing documentary of all time. His latest film project, *Sicko*, taps into our collective confusion and rage about the American health-care system, which is viewed by many to be overly complex and purely profit-driven. When four of the major pharmaceutical companies ordered their employees not to speak with Moore, this "shutdown" garnered massive press for Moore, including an article in the *Los Angeles Times* aptly entitled, "Drug Firms are on the Defense as Filmmaker Michael Moore Plans to Dissect Their Industry." Talk about turning a major setback into positive publicity!

What's Michael Moore's true secret? He creates outrage over things going on in our world that people are already upset or angry about, then takes facts, cold and seemingly objective statistics, and gets an audience personally attached. He brings home the facts by showing the people who have been directly affected by them. You'll either feel sympathy or disgust, but suddenly you *care* about the numbers and the statistics. Always play the human angle. How does your idea relate to everyday life? If you can't do this, your pitch has little chance of becoming a cultural firestarter. In *Sicko,* for example, Moore often steers clear of statistics. Instead, when he interviews a British doctor in hopes of seeing how well physicians are paid under a socialist medical system, he asks what he drives. He asks about other possessions—TVs, his house, and so forth. The image of a physician who owns a flat-screen television and drives a shiny new Audi is infinitely more telling than a lame chart of income breakdowns. It adds to the human element of his overall message.

★ 32

SECRET #4: THE TRUTH COUNTS . . . OR DOES IT?

Effective publicity whoring is grounded in the truth, but the best possible truth that can be found in your story. You're taking reality and making it more exciting! Going back to Sam Adams and his Boston Tea Party, there were probably less glamorous ways of dealing with the British tea tax. He could have taken a more legislative route, but that would have lacked the immediacy and word-of-mouth buzz the Tea Party ultimately generated. Instead, he did something dramatic and fascinating and helped spark a revolution.

There are, however, people out there who outright lie in order to get press coverage. I think of this as using the dark side of the Force—it may help at first, but it's not worth it in the long run.

Recently, a self-published author got a lot of online blog coverage—and a plug in the *New York Daily News*—after a rumor was started claiming that her book in some way upset actress Katie Holmes. Eventually, the truth came out: It was allegedly a hoax created by the author herself with a fake email message sent out to the gossip-blog editors. In reality, she was little more than a hack whom Holmes has never heard of!

While I now *know* about this author's work as a result of reading about her ploy on Gawker, I have no intention of seeking out her book. Publicity that makes the public even *less likely* to try your product or support your cause is not good publicity!

The secret to be learned from publicity missteps? Regardless of the details, you want your overall story or pitch to create a *positive* connection with your public. People should feel that you're a good person, an approachable company, an easy solution to their problems. Publicity that repulses people is undesirable; publicity that draws people in is absolutely golden.

Or has that rule, like so much else in the modern buzz world, become obsolete? James Frey, author of *A Million Little Pieces,* was controversial from the moment his book came out. The book deals with drug addiction and alcoholism in a blunt manner that was originally believed to be factually accurate. In 2005, the book was selected as an Oprah's Book Club pick and enjoyed massive sales as a result, having sold over two million copies. When a definitive report on TheSmokingGun.com, entitled *A Million*

Little Lies: Exposing James Frey's Fiction Addiction, was published in early January 2006 . . . well, essentially all hell broke loose!

The media fallout was tremendous, with every blog, large and small, regurgitating the evidence published in TSG's online report. You can still read the six-page take-down piece here: http://www.thesmokinggun.com/archive/0104061jamesfrey1.html. Frey's lawyer allegedly threatened the website with a multimillion-dollar lawsuit, but the damage had already been done. Frey stated, "So let the haters hate, let the doubters doubt, I stand by my book, and my life, and I won't dignify this bullshit with any sort of further response." Indeed, quite a few readers began to hate, including Oprah Winfrey.

Frey has since moved on to new projects, but the book continues to sell briskly and take up space in bookstores—now equipped with a "disclaimer" from the publisher. While the controversy has no doubt damaged his reputation within the publishing community, it keeps selling because *people are talking about it.* So is all publicity ultimately good publicity? I'll let you decide.

★ 34

SECRET #5: DEALING WITH PRESS STRESS

You should know this up front: Not all of your media coverage is going to be positive. While most reporters and producers are good people, they are human—and some of them have their own bones to pick. It never hurts to do your research ahead of time. Google the name of the newspaper reporter who will be interviewing you, and check out some of his or her stories. Make sure the stories seem unbiased and don't have a bizarre personal agenda.

Regardless of how much research you do, there are a few rare bad seeds in the media who get off on creating negative pieces. As the old newspaper saying goes, *"If it bleeds, it leads."* Villains sell more copies than good, hard-working citizens—and if turning you into a villain will make them more money, they just might do it. The best strategy here is to be fair in your dealings with others and to watch what you say during interviews. If you are incredibly paranoid about a certain reporter's track record, insist upon an email interview, and save your email records. That way no inaccurate quotes can be attributed to you.

The point here is this: **Not all press will be good.** Maintain a clear head and remember Rule #4: Take *nothing* personally. Even less-than-ideal press is better than no coverage at all. If people are talking about you, that means you matter. You'll have plenty of time to improve your public image. This does not contradict the previous section where I say that publicity missteps are to be avoided. When negative publicity is beyond your control, it is obviously not your fault. Use it to your advantage—a controversy can get more reporters interested in what you have to say. This is obviously a great chance to set the record straight.

★ Hugh Grant and Savvy Spin

Although this is now sliding into ancient history, you may remember Hugh Grant's run-in with a Hollywood hooker in 1995. The well-publicized blunder was certainly embarrassing, but it kept the limelight on Grant, and since then he has held lead roles in numerous acclaimed films. *Even if it seems bad, you can bounce back from it.* A CNN.com article from 1995 explains precisely why Grant was able to rise above the controversy: "Because of savvy spin control, Hugh Grant can be assured that his career will last more than nine months. By apologizing publicly, Grant has taught celebrities facing scandals in the future a lesson in how to defuse a crisis."

Here's his secret: Rather than hiding and letting the press endlessly speculate, he immediately came forward. Grant hit the talk-show circuit hard, apologizing everywhere and seemingly to everyone. The American public was flattered and quickly forgave him. Even though America can seem like a preposterously puritanical society at times, it really isn't—our movies are violent, our entertainment is drenched in sexual imagery (ask Britney Spears), and our politicians are far from squeaky clean. What people dislike is being lied to, because it is insulting. If you get caught in a sticky situation, come clean early. If the past is any indication, the scandal might even *help* your career in the long run.

As long as you're a good person and treating people with respect, you'll be alright in the long run. Malicious reporters are few and far between—when you do get a negative piece or review, don't fixate on it. Focus on all of the positive press you're receiving, and move on with your campaign.

Be brave and think long-term. Look at the blockbuster franchise films playing at your local cinema for inspiration.

Many of the highest-grossing movies initially get *ripped* by the critics. Does that bar a movie from an amazing opening weekend? In almost all cases, the answer is no.

SECRET #6: THE MEDIA IS FOR PROFIT

This isn't a media studies book, so I'm not going to delve into the implications of a capitalistic "free" press. Much like your first time at a casino, the less you know about what motivates media companies, the better. You'll encounter beginner's luck this way.

But still, it does help to know the main truth behind all media: Media companies exist primarily to make money; television producers exist to find and develop stories that attract viewers and in turn make money for the show. Online media companies are basically the same. Whereas TV networks want viewers, websites want clicks. They aren't in the business of helping you out or making you famous. When these things happen, it is a byproduct. Create a compelling, exciting message—something that producers think will lure in viewers—and you can be sure that you'll get coverage.

There is also a nonprofit sector of the American media—NPR, PBS, and some independently run radio talk shows. Also, there are nonprofit blogs run by people with nothing better to do. However, these media outlets still want a compelling story. They may be less vulnerable to hyperbole and hype, but they love to discover a convincing story. Nonprofit radio lends itself well to exploring human-interest stories, because they don't have to worry about commercial breaks or losing listeners.

SECRET #7: PEOPLE WILL CRITICIZE—AND THAT'S FREE PUBLICITY

Just as not all press will be good, not every person is going to become an overnight fan. It is unfortunate, but some people find pleasure in criticizing others. Part of this behavior is definitely the result of jealousy: They see you on TV or hear you on the radio making your dreams a reality. This upsets people, especially those with aspirations similar to yours who aren't making it happen.

There's a secret to keep in mind here: Instead of trying to win over the 5 percent of people who don't like you and probably *never* will, why not focus your energy on the other 95 percent who love what you're doing? Online criticism, in particular, is something that affects even the most talented celebrities. No one is immune to a splash of "Haterade" from time to time.

In an indirect way, negative online comments from blog readers and subscribers actually *help* you. Controversy keeps a story active for longer—blog editors are more likely to run more items on you or your company if they notice a visceral reaction from readers. The thing a blogger fears most? Publishing a post and seeing *(0) new comments* directly below it. If people are trashing you online in the user comments sections of magazines and blogs, this is not a big deal: Nobody takes these back alleys of the Web seriously. User comments are often overtly ignorant and poorly spelled diatribes. Yet, despite this, it is an indicator of how much impact an item has on a blog's readers.

Head over to TMZ.com sometime and see what I mean: A fairly uneventful post may have only a handful of user comments, while a major breaking story or controversial item can fetch five hundred or more comments in a very short period of time.

While comments are not taken seriously by anyone who matters, they can stoke the buzz flames. A particularly vicious user comment will, in turn, coax supporters of your company or you into writing something positive. In choosing sides, people start to feel "attached" to you—and they want to see your product or cause succeed. Try dissing someone's favorite actor in casual conversation or downplaying the usefulness of an iPod to someone who owns one. It won't fly; you'll get a serious reaction.

SECRET #8: OVERCOMING PUBLICITY POSTPARTUM DEPRESSION

Knowing When and Where to Find the Next Hook

We're going to learn how to get your campaign massive attention—that's the easy part. The hard part is knowing when to let go. There comes a point in every publicity whore's campaign when he must realize it's over and it's time to move onto something newer and better.

True publicity masters don't permanently define themselves with any single cause or buzz campaign. Get your press, profit from it, and find a new cause. The media is *always* looking for the next thing. If you can become a reliable source of new stories, this is far more valuable than a one-time stunt.

There is no rule against reinventing yourself on a regular basis. Look at artists, both historically and in modern times. The impressionist painters drastically varied their work over time. Almost every noted writer's work evolves over time. Pop icon Madonna has stayed famous for more than twenty years and remains culturally relevant by reinventing herself. The Madonna you hear on the radio now is *not* the same artist you heard back in 1982.

Expert buzz whores know this secret: It's not only okay to change, it's absolutely *imperative.* Even the most intriguing hook will not keep the media's attention for more than a few days or a couple weeks at most. When one of your favorite authors comes out with a tempting new novel, how long does her work stay in the public eye? Usually, assuming the author is nationally known, she hits the TV and radio circuit for only a matter of days. You see her on one morning television show and then hear her laughing on the radio the following evening. By next week, the show bookers have moved onto other authors and actors.

Know your story's shelf life, and be prepared to pounce on the next hot topic.

CHAPTER 3

All Fires Start with a Spark:
Getting Friendly with Mean Bloggers

"Blogger" is perhaps one of the most unpleasant and goofy names imaginable. Despite this, those who write for a living on the Internet (and those who write for the hell of it—the vast majority) play a crucial role in the growth of any buzz campaign. A blog is an online personal journal with all sorts of information from the author, stories about his or her life, product recommendations, thoughts on the current political situation—anything you can think of, someone has blogged about it. And as pedestrian as it may sound, millions of people read and comment on blogs every day.

What makes a blog different from other media formats, and distinct from other online outlets, is the ease with which the author of a blog can create updates. A blog need not be a long discourse on a social issue; it can also be a quick three-line analysis of a breaking news story. It can be a link to a funny YouTube video with a sentence urging visitors to check it out. Of course, it can also be an intelligent essay or important journalistic narrative. Blogs typically categorize posts chronologically, with the newest content toward the top. The blog is an innovative, unpredictable media format that is likely here to stay.

Unless you have an extensive list of media contacts, and even if you do, blog mentions are often the best way to attract mainstream media attention. Blogs are like a farming system for stories. A blog runs something; if it's a compelling story, it grows through online word of mouth, and other blogs start to cover it. Eventually, sometimes within hours, television and radio producers will jump on the story.

And getting attention from radio and TV outlets needn't always be the aim of a blog mention: Some online publications have significant readerships. Plus the online format obviously has several advantages over an offline plug. Imagine a popular syndicated radio talk show host, carried on *hundreds* of stations around the country, gives your cause a thirty-second mention and plugs your website. That's an amazing amount of exposure, right? Yes, it may be, but how many of his listeners are going to write down your URL while they are driving to work? How many are going to remember you at all after listening to the host chat for the next twenty minutes? How many are going to care about you after the entertaining celebrity guest does a phone-in interview? The point is that people have short attention spans, and if your cause is advertised in a medium that means they'll have to perform an action to get to you—like remember your URL and log in—they're probably not going to do it.

With a blog mention, things are a little different. Blog visitors read the post about your cause and often have the option of clicking right to your website from the story, right then and there, before they lose interest. Also, the blogging "community" is tight-knit in many ways and feeds off of itself. One blog will link to another blog's story and then add a bit of additional commentary. This furthers word-of-mouth buzz, because people will see your story many places and think it's hot. Plus, blog posts are somewhat permanent forms of publicity. Three months from now, a person searching on Google could come across the blog post about your cause and click on it. A journalist looking for you on Google News would be able to get more background information.

SECRET #9: MAKE YOUR OWN BLOG

Creating a blog is super easy. The two main hosted applications, **Blogger.com** and **TypePad.com**, are both simple to use, even for the computer illiterate. Blogging serves several purposes. It is a great way to build free search-engine traffic. It's also a great way to build a fan base, especially if your publicity style is focused on your personality.

Even if your publicity campaigns are focused more on your product or business than on you as a personality, blogging offers interested people constant updates on you and your campaign. Back in the day, an online newsletter could accomplish this, but now many email users will delete anything that has a publicity angle. We're so tired of spam in our in-boxes, we toss anything that sounds even remotely commercial!

A blog allows your customers or fans to interact with you on their own terms. They view your updates when *they* have the time, not when you feel like sending out an email to everyone. And they can post real-time comments sharing their feedback with you. Including your blog URL in a press release is often a great idea, as it will provide interested reporters with more background information about you.

Don't rule out publishing a blog right on MySpace: This will make it easier for your existing social network "friends" to view your newest entries, as links to them will be placed directly opposite a photo of you on your profile page. (If you aren't familiar with MySpace, the service is explained in Chapter 3).

LiveJournal.com is another solid, free blog provider worth checking out: Signing up is hassle-free, and the blog network already has a massive number of registered users, meaning you will have a built-in audience of potential readers.

Also consider newcomer **Tumblr.com**, arguably the easiest and fastest of the new blogging services. It takes literally around thirty seconds to create a personalized blog over there, and the already designed templates are all quite snazzy looking.

Regardless of which blog service you end up using, here's a secret: Create an appropriate title. As we discussed earlier, you want your title field to be rich with keywords visitors will use to find you on search engines. For example, if I were creating a blog for this book from scratch, "David's Blog" or "David's Home-page" would be terrible title choices. Instead, I would create a title such as "How to Become Famous, Dynamic Fame, Celebrity Interviews, Buzz—David Seaman." This way, anyone searching for me by name would see my blog as a top search result on Google. Additionally, bored surfers looking for celebrity interviews and ways to "become famous" would be exposed to my blog as well. This is highly targeted traffic: If a person visiting my blog is already interested in celebrity culture, he or she is likely to take an interest in this book. Get it? Good.

ZACH BRAFF'S SYNDICATED SUPERBLOG

Zach Braff's blog (http://zachbraff.com) is the epitome of the commercialized personal blog. The actor/director has each of his posts syndicated through LiveJournal and MySpace for maximum coverage. Also, despite his popularity, he allows visitors to comment on each post—with a promise that he actually takes the time to read them all! On MySpace alone, Braff has over *269,000* friends (http://myspace.com/zachbraff). Most of his posts hawk his upcoming films and *Scrubs* episodes, but there's also the occasional peek into his personal life. A personal blog, if used with commercial intent, can have a *tremendous* impact. Braff is reportedly now one of the highest-paid actors in television, raking in more than US $300,000 per episode. It certainly doesn't hurt to have a legion of loyal blog fans!

Roscoe Braff

Not only does Zach Braff have his own significant MySpace presence; he has a MySpace profile (http://myspace.com/roscoebraff) for his *dog*, Roscoe. **The secret here? Build loyalty at any cost, even if it means opening yourself up a bit.** I personally don't care to read about a television actor's pet, but there are evidently plenty of people out there (most of them presumably young) who *do* care about such things. Give people more than enough information and access to you. In this day and age, where everything is only a few keystrokes away, it makes no sense to appear aloof. Open yourself up; let people in. If you're a company, make your customers feel like they are in on the secret (whatever it may be). Giving information provides a sort of modern intimacy—as long as you aren't posting material that is detrimental to you, of course!

★ Fake-Blog Buzz Creation

Some people create blogs for the sole purpose of promoting their causes in the third person. This is extraordinarily lame, and most blog visitors, who tend to be savvy consumers of information, will spot your con a mile away and automatically dismiss whatever you have to say.

If you create a blog, own up to it. Don't make it seem like a blog is "covering" a story about you. Also, there is something known as blog spamming (blamming?), which we don't really need to discuss, other than to say it's ineffective. Creating a hundred blogs that talk about your cause is not going to get you attention. A single mention on a widely read blog will, however, so let's discuss how to pull that off! But first, a closer look at the unintentionally humorous world of blog spamming.

In a nutshell, programs exist that launch hundreds of blogs, each chock-full of keywords you may search for on Google or another search engine. When you visit the page, it is little more than gibberish and a lot of text ads targeted to match whatever keywords are on the web page. It's super lame, it's ineffective, and search engines are now thankfully cracking down on this weird little sub-industry.

Now, as for individual fake blogs, it is actually a more common occurrence to see them in support of particular companies and products. While pointing any fingers here would likely lead to a lawsuit, be wary of any blog whose sole purpose is gushing about how amazing a particular product is—especially if the blog is absent of any negative user comments whatsoever. Negativity is widespread in user comment sections, as we discussed earlier. If it's absent, something is fishy!

SUCCESSFUL, FUNNY FAKE BLOGS

On a lighter note, the fake blog phenomenon known as Fake Steve Jobs is worth mentioning. Titled *The Secret Diary of Steve Jobs* (http://fakesteve.blogspot.com/), this imaginative blog is published by a guy who "pretends" to be Apple's chief executive officer, Steve Jobs. Luckily, most of the blog's readers are in on the longstanding joke. He posts new entries simply as "Steve," with a quirky profile description that succinctly reads: "I love beautiful objects. I love creating them. Negative people upset me."

This bizarre online falsity has resulted in a real book deal for Fake Steve. The book, *Options* (Da Capo Press, 2007), is getting rave reviews so far. As *Entertainment Weekly* put it: "Just as Tom Wolfe skewered Wall Street in the '80s, Fake Steve Jobs lights a mini-*Bonfire* in Silicon Valley with *Options.*"

Men Who Look Like Old Lesbians (http://menwho looklikeoldlesbians.blogspot.com/) is another inane idea that has taken off in the blogosphere. Widely written about and linked to from high-traffic sites such as Kottke.org and social bookmarking site Digg.com, the blog has only one aim: Publishing photos of famous men who, in some unfortunate photographs, may appear to look a bit like . . . well, you know, old lesbians. I mention this only to remind you that the world of blogs is truly bizarre and often unpredictable.

SECRET #10: ANATOMY OF A BLOGGER

Contrary to the image of a blogger in his underwear, posting updates from Mom's basement when he's not hitting reload on the Craig's List "casual encounters" page, many bloggers these days are paid professionals. They are increasingly employed by media companies, either the online arms of conglomerates or relatively new online upstarts. Even old-guard, established publications such as the *New York Times* and *USA Today* are now heavily involved in the development of regular blog features.

Whatever the reason for their writing, bloggers have the same motivation as anyone else on the Internet: They want compelling stories that will generate clicks. They want to post items that cubicle slaves bored at work will forward to their friends, IM link to, and so forth. Basically, their sole purpose is to generate buzz about something—and that something might as well be you and your idea.

SECRET #11: HOW TO GET A BLOG MENTION

Most blogs will have their contact information, usually a tip-line or general email address, visible on their sites' home-pages. Send your pitch to this address. You can either send a blind pitch, which may or may not get you coverage on the blog, or you can respond to content already on the blog.

For example, in 2007, a massive online furor started over footballer Michael Vick's involvement in dog fighting. If you were offended by his actions, you could write a pitch that interacted with that issue in some way, possibly how you raised your own dogs, to show how inhumane Vick's actions were. You would have a great hook if you were a veterinarian—you could write about the injuries to the dogs. If you were a business owner, you could announce that you're giving a donation to the local SPCA. I'm not suggesting philanthropy for the sake of buzz; I'm just suggesting pitches that *relate* to touchstone issues. It makes you relevant to the blog, as opposed to being yet another self-promoter desperate for coverage.

Tying in with a hot-button issue builds buzz for you because as long as the topic is hot, you are a part of the discussion. Your quote will be used in news stories around the world, and you'll become something of an "expert" on the issue by default. Radio shows, desperate for people who are close to the issue and affected by it, will invite you on.

Here's a pitch secret: Never use "boilerplate" pitches. In other words, if your pitch is the same regardless of the recipient, you are not doing it right. Each pitch should be specific to the blog you are writing to, and it should be written in "plain language," not in ad-speak. This means it should be very close to a personal letter. If your pitch is filled with links to your websites and hyperbole about how your product is great, it will be overlooked. Bloggers are swamped with materials from corporate publicists—if you want to be noticed, appear to be a genuine human. Just explain why an issue impacts you; then, in the next couple sentences, explain how you feel about it. Be forceful: You want to include at least one interesting quote that the editor can actually use in an upcoming story. Before closing, mention your credentials, product, and website address. This should be an afterthought, not the main thrust of your message. This way, you are primarily offering something of value to the editor, and then giving him or her the option of plugging you.

Include a phone number where you can be reached—nine times out of ten the editor will be too busy to follow up with a telephone call, but it lends a degree of authenticity anyway. Plus, occasionally an editor *will* call for more details, and this can only mean a more substantial role for you in the post.

★ Blog Burnout

Can you get too much blog coverage? Once you're "picked up" by a major blog in a certain niche, it is possible that other blogs covering the same niche or industry will write about you as well. Blog visitors are somewhat promiscuous and read numerous blogs, so they'll see your name over and over again. They'll become familiar with you and your cause.

For 99.9 percent of individuals and causes, this is not a problem—even with substantial blog coverage, the editors will move onto a new topic soon. However, for causes that are personality-driven, where the blogs will be discussing *you* as a person, burnout can become an issue. Blog visitors will grow annoyed with you. "*Why are you such a big deal?!*" they'll wonder aloud in the comments section. This is particularly true in cases where a person rises quickly. Patrick Moberg, who saw a girl on the subway whom he instantly fell for and created a website called NYGirlofMyDreams.com in the hopes of finding her, received a storm of online (and television) press. At first amusing to the bored masses, he soon became an object of ridicule, with many questioning his motivations—entirely innocent, or a blatant grab for Internet stardom?

Of course, the next question is whether you should even care. If people start posting comments asking about you and why you're getting blog coverage, then you are generating controversy. The controversy will grow and grow until you have thousands of blog readers eagerly devouring new posts about you, all the while lamenting the fact that you're getting so much coverage! It's an absurd vicious circle, and one you should be prepared to milk for all it's worth.

NATALIE REID'S BLOG BUZZ

Natalie Reid moved to New York from Canada in hopes of making it as a model. Fashion photographers continuously told her that she bears a striking resemblance to Paris Hilton. This initially annoyed Reid and at times made getting work difficult, until she decided to embrace the similarity and use it as a strength.

Today, Natalie is known all over the world as the "Paris Hilton look-alike"—she was a contestant on ABC's celebrity look-alike show, *The Next Best Thing*, and has been profiled by a wide variety of international media.

What's interesting about her is that she benefits greatly from online buzz without herself owning or editing a blog. Celebrity gossip blogs like TMZ provide her with valuable free coverage, but it comes at a price. The user comments on such sites are notoriously mean and underhanded. How does she deal?

"They see you as this superhero: Where they admire you and desire to be like you, although they know they never can be.... You are a fantasy, and this puts a lot of pressure on people that are in the public eye," she told me. Once you start getting a certain amount of national media coverage, some will see you as a fantasy and not as a real person—learn to deal with callous comments from people you've never even met!

SECRET #12: TAKE ADVANTAGE OF SLOW NEWS CYCLES

Television, radio, and print outlets all experience slow news cycles—times when seemingly nothing major is occurring in the world. These happen a lot during the summer, especially in August, when very little political controversy is brewing. The powerful and assorted news-makers of the day are on vacation. As a result, many blogs experience a lull in stories—since most blogs respond to stories reported by other outlets and build upon them with the author's interpretation and impressions, they need an instigator to write about. Of course, blogs also break stories of their own, but the majority of the time they rely on newsmakers for their material.

★ 54

There's a secret to be learned here: Take advantage of slow news cycles. When a blog seems to be struggling to find new content, and *especially* if the blog's editors start to openly complain about how slow things are, use that window of opportunity to send in a pitch. A lot of less-than-primetime pitches will make their way onto blogs during a slow cycle, as long as you're fresh and original.

I'm not saying your pitch can be less than perfect; I'm just saying that an "unknown" person or organization has a better shot at coverage during a slow cycle. To get a feel for what I'm talking about in this chapter, I've included some real-life examples below. Learn from their successes and failures.

MOBY'S ALIENATING BLOG

If you have a blog, you should try to self-edit before you post things. Ask yourself if what you're about to post to the Internet, where the whole world can see it, is really something that will improve your public image. If the answer to that question is a definite no, don't post it.

The musician Moby runs a blog on his website that, in all likelihood, alienates a portion of his fans. He regularly posts about absurdly trivial matters and complains about the various "stresses" of being a musician on tour—lack of sleep being one repeat offender. Also, much of the blog has a political bent, which is okay . . . but there's no way for visitors to add their comments! If you are going to post polarizing political views, at least let your visitors chime in. Keep them involved.

The secret here is about loyalty. If you let your public in on your life—which I recommend you do—make sure you are showing your best side. Don't complain about how last quarter you had so much business that you had to spend the weekend packing orders. Don't write long posts explaining to your fans what a "hassle" it is to be famous. Keep your blog posts relentlessly upbeat; it will keep people coming back. Make people proud to be a part of your personal or business success. Get

55 | ★

> good mentions on other blogs in any reasonable manner (seriously—be reasonable), but on your own blog make sure you portray yourself as the person you want others to see. It's the only place online where you can control your image!

★ Julia Allison's Online Fame

New York dating columnist Julia Allison has a flamboyant and provocative personality that has made her the subject of numerous gossip blog postings in recent years. Through a combination of skill and luck, Julia has catapulted herself to national media prominence. Over time, she has positioned herself as a talkative celebrity news pundit, and her blog (http://juliaallison.com) keeps readers up to date on her newest projects—and some areas of her personal life. She's *Star Magazine*'s former editor-at-large and runs a dating column in *Time Out New York*. It is estimated that she made as many as 250 television appearances in 2007 alone.

When she showed up to be interviewed for this book, she was wearing a bright yellow dress and her face had a slightly orange glow. (Fresh out of a morning television appearance, she hadn't yet found time to wipe off the makeup.)

If you're a morning TV addict, it is almost impossible to go a week without seeing Julia. She's frequently on *Fox & Friends, The Today Show,* and many other a.m. chatterfests. One of the things that immediately struck me about Julia, aside from her confidence, was an almost encyclopedic knowledge of what other well-known people were doing. More specifically, people who had risen to fame in a dynamic or underground way.

"Have you interviewed Obama Girl yet? You need to interview her," she said. Aside from her fascination with the celebrity culture, and her belief that there is a "direct correlation" between fame and influence on others (I agree), Julia is interested in the concept of *credibility*. I would use the word authenticity: What you're saying on blogs, what you're mentioning on radio shows, and so forth should have a more or less consistent feel. People should grow to trust you.

"Paris Hilton is *screwed*," she explained to me. Basically, her argument was that recognition alone is never enough. Yes, in the short term you can endorse products and "sell shit," but credibility is crucial. People don't necessarily trust anything Paris Hilton says; it comes across as superficial or contrived.

Aside from the items written about Julia Allison on gossip blogs, the fact that she edits her own blog to keep fans posted on upcoming television appearances is crucial. For those who missed certain shows, she provides screen-shots and funny recaps. Also, her blog is at times self-deprecating and endearing. In a recent post in which she recommended books to her *Time Out New York* column's readers, she wrote, "Like Oprah's [Book Club] but instead of the power to rocket your book to the *NYT* Bestseller List, the power to . . . uh . . . rocket your book to . . . uh. . . yeah, pretty much no power at all." This is what blogging is all about; creating interest and then winning people over with a specific voice. It lets someone emerging as a public personality let their guard down and allows for real communication with fans.

Her blog keeps her relevant: It becomes primary source material for gossip blogs—in a sense, Julia Allison's blog has made *her* a story, rather than just the celebrities she dishes about on-air. This is important because it "diversifies" her image: She isn't tied to any one news story in particular. Instead, she is discussed as a personality.

Where This Is Headed: Julia Allison Gets It

 This is email I received from Julia Allison a few weeks after interviewing her. I had asked her if she had any additional thoughts on social networking and dynamic fame. What she says makes a lot of sense!

Subject: On Dynamic Fame

First, let's define Famous. Famous, adj "known by many people." So how is being known by many people helpful?

Well, it must be. Otherwise, why the hell do VH1 & E! exist?!

If there were no evolutionary benefit to fame, no one would chase it—or certainly not as doggedly as they do now. To be well-known gives many people (perhaps most people?) pleasure, and generally things that give us pleasure have their roots in something

---

that at one point helped us. There could be no other reason for the proliferation and (exponentially accelerating) mass obsession with fame.

Ultimately, I think it has something to do with the fact that people will DO things for you if you're famous or well-known. It's a type of power. So let's say, back in the day, you were famous amongst your little tribe, well, people would be more likely to bring you back nuts & berries & shit. They'd be more likely to give you the better cave, the better cave women, the better spot in the hunting pack, whatever (I hate these stupid "back in the cave days" examples, but still, I can't think of anything better). Thus, fame was a type of currency very early on.

In any case, how does this relate to web fame? Well . . .

Fame is funny. If you REALLY think about it, it doesn't MATTER whether you're famous throughout the entire world, like Brad Pitt, or all of America, like Mandy Moore, or famous just at your college, or famous in your chosen career (maybe you're the most famous electrician in Des Moines!) In any of these cases, you're going to accrue the benefits of fame—the adulation, the sense of false familiarity, the reassurance that people you don't know personally will treat you well and help you out when you need something.

As long as you're surrounded by people who think you're famous, it doesn't matter where they are. So the web, in a sense, has created billions of heretofore nonexistent opportunities for people to become famous in their own niches—whereas before they were limited to real-world communities.

One more thing—the Internet also leads many people to believe they are famous and, as such, begin acting in fame-addled ways. As anyone who is familiar with E! or the celebrity newsweeklies knows, fame often goes hand in hand with rampant and unrestrained egotism. Rosie O'Donnell explained the phenomenon quite well:

"It is a shift that happens in the head and that very few celebrities will ever really speak about.... One begins to believe in the specialness, and a dangerous sense of entitlement takes over.... When celebrity addiction starts, you become impatient with, and even angry at necessary obstacles. You think you could run a red light or two. And then you do."

Therefore, due to the Internet, a huge (and growing) number of people have acquired what a good friend of mine termed "situational narcissism."

In terms of whether online tools like Facebook were valuable in creating dynamic fame, I'd say of course, in certain ways they were invaluable. Namely, they facilitated dynamic fame amongst smallish cybergroups that would never have formed otherwise. But it's important to note that while they were accessories to the crime, they were not the genesis. The genesis was the Internet in and of itself, the Internet as a medium with which to display and familiarize personalities. Prior to the Internet, your options for achieving fame were as follows: acting, athletics, politics, royalty, or sure, you could get a little attention by killing a few people in a dramatic way. Other than that, you were probably doomed to the dim twilight that knows neither MySpace nor YouTube.

Now, on the other hand, you need merely a T1 line and a digital camera and three days from now, you could sit opposite Matt Lauer on the *Today Show* as ten million people watch you give the director's commentary on your poorly lit, badly edited three-minute viral video.

Welcome to Dynamic Fame! The anarchy which, at its most delusional, believes itself to be a meritocracy.

61 ★

SECRET #13: THE MAJOR BLOGS

Below, you'll find a quick run-through of the major blogs on the Internet—get familiar with these blogs and start to read them. Get a feel for the sorts of stories they run, and then pitch the ones that feel right to you. Don't be a nuisance; pitch with ideas that actually *add* to the discussion on these blogs or include information that will be useful to the blog's audience. And, naturally, try to pitch during a slow news cycle!

Gawker.com

In several short years, Gawker has gone from obscure "Manhattan media" gossip to a destination blog for thousands of daily readers—many of whom are influential TV producers and magazine editors (who view the site, in part, to make sure they aren't being made fun of on it!).

TMZ.com

Short for the "thirty-mile zone" that defines the Hollywood area, this site is focused almost entirely on celebrity gossip—although it occasionally will give press to something that is just plain bizarre. TMZ is essentially the CNN of the gossip blogosphere, and it is actually part owned by the same company as CNN. The blog is increasingly video-oriented and is difficult to pitch directly. Stories on other blogs eventually make their way onto TMZ if they have serious merit. (With that said, I've placed stories on TMZ, so it's definitely possible to appear there!)

Kottke.org

With more of a tech bent, Jason Kottke's site provides a list of outward links to various things of interest. Very popular.

Fark.com

Fark is a combination blog and link-sharing community. A "greenlighted" link on the site can easily receive twenty thousand or more visitors, so it's worth pitching.

Lifehacker.com

With a tech/lifestyle orientation, this is one to pitch if your story appeals to a technology-savvy crowd.

Engadget.com

An in-depth blog covering the latest mobile technologies and hottest new phone trends. Mobile devices are becoming increasingly popular; so are the blogs that cover this industry.

Consumerist.com

A popular site for bored, overly vigilant consumers. A lot of the coverage can be negative—keep that in mind if you want to pitch them, and tailor to their style.

63 ★

TVNewser.com

TV Newser is a blog covering the television news industry. Great blog to watch—it will give you a good, accurate feel for the TV news world and the outlandish personalities who run it.

Galleycat.com

Blog covering the publishing community. Also another good blog to watch, and it is possible to appear on there if your pitch is subtle.

Jossip.com

A New York-area gossip blog. Easy to pitch.

Gothamist.com

Gothamist is yet another New York regional blog, but it is widely read and covers many aspects of the city such as entertainment and dining—not just gossip.

Defamer.com

A Los Angeles-area gossip blog focusing on the film industry and the usual celebrity chatter. The site has enjoyed numerous high-profile plugs, including mentions on *Nip/Tuck* and *Entourage.*

Jezebel.com

A celebrity and fashion gossip blog specifically for female readers.

DailyKos.com

A liberal-leaning political blog—extremely popular.

HuffingtonPost.com

Arianna Huffington's popular online political publication, with numerous bloggers publishing new content to the site on a regular basis.

Wonkette.com

A blog covering political news in Washington.

BigHeadDC.com

Another Washington political blog, growing in popularity and delightfully aggressive in its pursuit of exclusive information.

The Medium (http://themedium.blogs.nytimes.com)

The Medium is a *New York Times* blog that sees its beat as the online viral video world. From the blog's profile: "With television and the Internet converging at last, who's going to watch all this here-goes-nothing online video? Everything from political propaganda videos to pseudo-candid celebrity rants seems to expect an audience. *The Medium* will find, review and make sense of all those senseless new images . . . "

Tech_Space (http://blogs.usatoday.com/techspace/)

Tech_Space, a *USA Today* blog, contains "daily notes on science and silicon"—in reality, the blog's scope is fairly large, so try pitching anything that can relate to a tech-savvy audience.

i09.com

i09, as it is called, is a brand-new science fiction and sci-fi culture blog. Seems like a small niche until you consider the number of people who watch the Sci-Fi Channel, attend Trekkie conventions, and casually try to use *Star Wars* quotes in everyday conversation. There are a staggering number of sci-fi fans out there, and they tend to be tech-savvy.

Slashdot.org

Immensely popular, collaborative technology news blog. A link on the Slashdot homepage can send a flood of website traffic in a short period of time.

MetaFilter.com

MetaFilter, or MeFi as the regulars on there call it, is a high-traffic collaborative blog and online community. The community's interests are varied; almost anything will fly as long as it is interesting or new.

CollegeHumor.com

Although more of an entertainment portal than a blog, CollegeHumor allows outsiders to submit articles and content for consideration. If they like it, they'll post it, and they will sometimes pay for original content. I've been published there before—it's a great place to get coverage (if you can!), because the site gets 200 *million* pageviews per month. Keep your submission funny, college-oriented, and relatively short.

SECRET #14: SOCIAL BOOKMARKING SITES:
The Backdoor Approach

Getting gossip-blog coverage ultimately depends on the whim of the human being on the other end of your pitch. If the editor doesn't like your idea, or if it doesn't fit the blog's audience, you're out of luck. Social bookmarking sites, on the other hand, harness the so-called wisdom of the masses. If your website or story has viral potential, a social bookmarking service will give you the platform needed for rapid buzz.

Basically, a social bookmark site is a network of users who submit links to sites or stories that they find interesting. The most "worthy" links rise to the top of the queue based on a number of factors—normally how many other people have linked to the item recently and how other users on the site rank it.

Buzz secret: You should have *everyone* within your organization sign up for social bookmarking accounts. If your "organization" consists of just you, then have your friends and family sign up for accounts. Then, when you're ready, have them all submit a link to your site around the same time. Your link will get catapulted to the front of the link queue, and if it has any viral potential, other users will start to recommend it and add the link to their own bookmarks list.

Sound confusing? It really isn't! Just go to http://del.icio.us, http://reddit.com, or http://digg.com. Those are the major three players at the moment. All services function more or less the same but have unique ways of doing things. I personally prefer Reddit because it has remained the easiest to understand (and thus easiest to manipulate!).

Under no circumstances should you sign up for multiple accounts yourself. You may think you're being sneaky, but these sites use IP logging and cookie caching to catch people artificially inflating interest in certain links. The only way to succeed is to have your friends submit your link around the same time as you. And, naturally, your site or story has to be something interesting. Otherwise it won't reach critical mass and rise to the top of the list.

Here's another killer secret: Analyze the top links on Del.icio.us, Reddit, and Digg. Try to figure out exactly why each one has become so popular. Within a few weeks you'll develop the uncanny ability to spot which new links are likely to take off. For example, anything related to open-source technology, libertarian politics, or a high-tech scandal is likely to do well on Reddit. Anecdotally, Reddit users tend to be the most "nerdy"—to such an extent that some general-audience viral items will not do well on the site. Del.icio.us has a fairly broad user base (and the site is now owned by Internet giant Yahoo!), so almost anything viral potentially can do well there. Digg is structurally the most advanced of the social bookmarking sites, categorizing content into three categories (news article, video, or image) and promoting it accordingly. Viral videos have the potential to do very well on Digg, but the site's audience is also interested in politics and tech stories.

Del.icio.us allows you to tag your submissions with relevant keywords—this means you can attach keywords to your story, so that when people run those words through search engines, they'll get a link to your story. You should definitely take advantage of this feature, because within a few days your posts will appear on Google and other search engines, and you'll start getting a lot more hits independently from Del.icio.us.

If you aren't entirely sure how all this can benefit you, flip ahead to my interview with Obama Girl on page 81. Her short YouTube video, a sexy ode to presidential candidate Barack Obama, is the very definition of a viral link. It's been viewed over nine million times and has received significant coverage from the U.S. television media. The social bookmarking sites certainly helped her video, and many others like it, gain a wider audience.

SECRET #15: PINGING SERVICES

At the risk of becoming too technical, you want to make sure that blog search engines know the *instant* you add anything new to your personal or professional blog. The reason for this is simple: Blog search engines often rank items by date added.

After you make any changes to your blog or add a new post, visit the Google Blog Search ping utility at http://blogsearch.google.com/ping/ and type in your blog address. Pinging services such as this will check for new posts automatically and index them quickly. Also pay a visit to Ping-o-matic! on a regular basis; you can find it at http://pingomatic.com and it's free to use. Just enter your blog URL, and the service will automatically notify Technorati, Weblogs.com, Feed Burner, My Yahoo!, and so forth. This will help get each new blog post as much visibility as humanly possible!

CHAPTER 4

MySpace, Facebook, and the Social Networking Revolution

MySpace.com is one of the most powerful buzz marketing tools at your disposal—and it's completely free. In a
matter of minutes you can create a profile for your business or cause, target the appropriate demographic in a
search, and begin networking with people who will
spread the word about you. MySpace, if you aren't
already familiar with it, allows you to create an online
profile complete with photos of you, video content, and
information on your various interests (favorite movies,
books, television programs, and so on). The service links
you to others' profiles if you request to become "friends"
with them.

MySpace was originally conceived as a way for bands to
make friends with music lovers and build their fan bases,
but the site has since evolved into a general-audience social
networking site. Part virtual business meeting, part trashy
dating site, and part online photo album, MySpace is a
major player in the online buzz world.

However, MySpace rival Facebook.com is quickly
becoming "the new MySpace." People intimately trust a
new message received on Facebook—as opposed to
MySpace, which has become overrun with
advertisements—and the service is just as easy to use.
While MySpace started as a scrappy band-networking
site, Facebook was originally founded by Harvard College
student Mark Zuckerberg as a way for college students to
network with each other. The name Facebook comes
from the "face books" that some colleges publish
containing photos of students with their contact

information. The site aimed to be an online equivalent, and it took off quickly.

Facebook has since expanded to allow anyone on the site, not just college students, but the service still enjoys considerable support on the college campuses where it first took hold. According to traffic ranking service Alexa, Facebook is currently the seventh most popular website on the Internet (MySpace is only slightly ahead at sixth).

Regardless of which site you decide to use (I recommend having a presence on both!), there are a few simple rules you need to follow to maintain your credibility while still getting the word out.

SECRET #16: RULES OF SOCIAL NETWORKING ETIQUETTE

1. Don't be overtly annoying. No wall posts or comments (messages on the front of someone's page) promoting your product or yourself. That's for amateurs. You're a buzz whore, not a spammer.

2. Think smart. Your profile text needs to jump out at the reader, your list of interests needs to reflect who you are as an individual or organization, your photos need to get people fascinated by whatever it is you do. Make your site a place that accurately reflects you and a page that people want to visit every day for updates.

3. Target aggressively! If your intended audience is guys in their mid-twenties, both MySpace and Facebook allow you to search for male users within a

certain age range. Take advantage of this by sending your information directly to them. Also, you can do an advanced search. Let's say you're an author with a New Age-y novella coming out. Friends have told you your writing style is similar to that of mega-bestseller Paulo Coelho. Do a search for users who list Paulo Coelho's *The Alchemist* in their favorite books section and friend them. Which brings us to the fourth and final rule...

4. "Friends" matter! Don't be shy about friending people on MySpace and Facebook. You want the numbers in your favor (in a moment, we'll talk about Tila Tequila and the power of having friends on these sites). You don't need to like everything about a person to be their MySpace buddy, and you certainly don't need to actually know them. If they're in your target demographic, you should be friends with them. It's that simple.

★ Tila Tequila and Her Million MySpace Friends

At the time of writing this, singer and model Tila Tequila now has over 2,016,000 friends on MySpace! When this chapter was first conceived, she had only half that number. This goes to show you how quickly things can take off on MySpace. Basic social dynamics state that people like to be friends with popular people. The same rule applies to the online world. This is *part* of the reason why it's crucial to have as many friends as possible on Facebook and MySpace.

The other reason is that these sites allow you to interact with your friends using bulletins and event notifications. Let's say you have 1,500 friends on Facebook, many of whom are interested in wine culture and live in the Southern California area. When your wine shop throws its monthly party, you can instantly notify these 1,500 people on Facebook using their event notification feature. Facebook will give you real-time information letting you know how many people plan on attending, how many are still undecided (you can send them a message encouraging them to check it out!), and how many are unable to attend. This is simply not possible with any other medium. Sure, you could paper your city with fliers about the wine shop party, but most people would ignore it, and the people you would attract might be weirdos! That's no way to effectively target your demographic. With Facebook, you know exactly who you've invited, and they're only those people whom you know are interested in what you're selling (in this case, wine aficionados in Southern California).

Online popularity definitely correlates to offline success. Tila Tequila has a platform so significant that MTV has given her a much-hyped dating reality show, *A Shot at Love with Tila Tequila.* The producers at MTV know that she has a potential built-in audience of two million people, thanks to her MySpace popularity. Those are two million people, many of them young (the vast majority of MySpace users are young), who are firmly within MTV's target audience. Also, Tila is bisexual, a fact MTV has exploited to the extreme by having both male and female contestants vie for her attention. The network has been not at all shy about promoting this fact. In promotional text on the MTV casting call web page, it describes the program as a "sexual stereotype shattering reality show" and Tila as a "gorgeous Bi-Bachelorette." The show is apparently popular enough that they are now casting participants for a second season! Just goes to show you that a powerful hook and a platform to deliver your message can make the difference between success and failure. The first season finale of Tila's show reportedly brought in an impressive 6.2 million viewers, "making it one of the most-watched cable telecasts of the week" and giving the "network its largest series audience ever," according to *E! News*.

★ 76

MySpace is the perfect platform-builder, which is why it's the home of so many musicians, comedians, and aspiring actors. It can be an online portfolio, audition reel, and buzz marketing tool rolled into one—be sure you use it, and use it wisely.

SECRET #17: BUILDING ONLINE STREET CRED

You don't want people to glance at your MySpace profile and immediately think "hack." For this reason, you should underplay your marketing activities and emphasize your personality. Tell people a bit about you as a company or person. Be colloquial, laid-back, genuine. In other words, don't make your MySpace profile sound like something concocted by a team of Madison Avenue advertising copywriters.

When you friend people, send them a personal message letting them know exactly why you friended them. As a marketer and buzz whore, it's your *job* to differentiate yourself from the other millions of people clamoring for attention on these sites. When you post something on another user's "wall" of comments, make it meaningful and personal. No "thanks for the add, check out our company site at . . . " Nobody will check it out, and you'll just seem desperate for clicks.

On Facebook, you can also now send personal messages to more than one recipient at once. This is perfect for new product announcements and assorted buzz-mongering activities. In addition, Facebook allows you to attach a brief video to the message you send out. Keep it to under fifteen or twenty seconds: Just a quick hello and intro. Put the rest of your content into the message itself. The reason for this is simple. Not everyone has a broadband connection, so don't make your video a long and annoying download. But it's refreshing to get a video message because so few people use that aspect of the site.

SECRET #18: COMMUNITY ADVERTISING ON FACEBOOK

For as little as five dollars, you can place a "flier" (basically a text ad) on Facebook that will be targeted based on network. So, for example, you could pay five dollars for a text ad to be shown only to users who attend Columbia University. If your product or message appeals to young people in a certain geographic region, Facebook advertising can be a quick way to reach them. Plus, advertising has a certain credibility, even in this age of constant commercials and nonsense. An ad is often perceived as more professional than a random wall post encouraging someone to check out your site. It's less intrusive; it's sanctioned and acceptable.

More recently, Facebook introduced a flier advertising system based on a cost per click (CPC) model. The CPC payment structure means you don't have to worry about creating text ads that are enticing. Your ad will be shown as many times as necessary to generate the desired number of clicks. You can also set how much you are willing to spend per click. Obviously, ads with a higher payment threshold are displayed more often.

I've tested this service and it works quite well for "quick" campaigns—campaigns you need to work immediately so they're relevant. You can set up an ad and have it running almost immediately. Gauge the results in real time and adjust your payment threshold accordingly—if you're not getting a lot of clicks, there's no reason to spend a lot for the extra exposure. Think about redefining your target audience if you're not generating a lot of interest—the service offers detailed demographic targeting at no additional cost (at least for now!). For example, you can specify that you want your ad to be shown only to single males between the ages of eighteen and twenty-four living in the United States. If your product is something that appeals to young single guys (deodorant mega-brands come to mind), this demographic targeting can be invaluable. You're only paying for clicks from users who may actually be interested in what you're offering.

Here's a secret: a lot of the time you need to be intuitive about who your cause or product should

be targeting. Unless you're a huge company, you may not have the resources to test who is most likely to respond well. Just make an educated guess, and then fill in your demographic targeting details. For instance, you may not have the numbers to factually prove that men ages eighteen to twenty-four in the United States are susceptible to advertisements for deodorant, but you know they need it. Market to them. Furthermore, Facebook allows you to target users based on their listed interests. So, if you are promoting an indie film that you think will go over well with fans of Kevin Smith movies, you could specifically target users who mention "Kevin Smith" or "*Clerks*" in their profiles. Kinda creepy, but fabulous from a buzz monger's point of view!

SECRET #19: SOCIAL NETWORKING AS A VIRAL PLATFORM 79 ★

With a few hundred friends on MySpace or Facebook, you can be sure that people are reading your profile and checking your bulletin updates. A bulletin is simply a notice simultaneously broadcast to all of your friends. The key is to use bulletins sparingly and only when you think a particular message will actually resonate with your "friends." If they find your cause funny or compelling, they will repost it to *their* friends. Count on this happening; pray for it! This is how online stars like Obama Girl and Chris "Leave Britney Alone!" Crocker are created—people spread the word. Best of all, it's free.

When I interviewed Obama Girl (real name: Amber Ettinger), she seemed in awe of the fact that something can spread *so* quickly. Although only in her early twenties, a single YouTube video has landed her as a guest or story on most of the major networks. The video featuring her scantily clad endorsement of Barack Obama for president has been viewed *millions* of times.

How much did this notoriety cost her? Absolutely nothing. If you create compelling content, it truly does become viral. You only need to let a few hundred people know about it, or at the most, a few thousand. Then it spreads. Whereas "word of mouth" used to result in someone *maybe* telling a friend or two about your cool idea, the new online viral world allows someone even *mildly* intrigued by your idea to tell absolutely everyone they know via MySpace or Facebook. This is extraordinarily powerful!

Chris Crocker's screechy defense of heartbreaking has-been Britney Spears on YouTube, imploring his viewers to just "Leave Britney Alone!!!," has been viewed over *eight million* times as of writing this. As Julia Allison explained to me, and this is a philosophy I agree with, notoriety leads to a kind of power—whether it be the power to endorse products, work on new projects, or become mainstream. In Crocker's case, he is now on the verge of a television deal, and 44 Blue Productions promises he *will* become an American TV star soon. It's a bizarre landscape, to be sure. **Although there's an element of luck in any runaway viral success, there's also a secret to be learned from past Internet stars: Be outrageous!**

Beyond outrageous, you need to be almost *unbelievable.* Another phenomenally popular viral video, which has landed on CNN and many other news programs, is the "Don't tase me, bro!" fiasco. In 2007, a college student was heckling Senator John Kerry as he gave a speech at the University of Florida. This college student was "escorted" out by security, but when he resisted, the dude yelled out, "Don't tase me, bro!" to the officers restraining him. Despite his request, this bro got Tasered, and luckily someone was there to record the hilarity on camera. It hit the Internet, as these things do, and now this guy has become a national punchline.

AN EMAIL FROM OBAMA GIRL

So where do I begin? :)

Ben Relles, who is the creator of barelypolitical.com, approached me with the concept after seeing my website amberleeonline.com.

81 ★

We met and he played me the song which was sung by Leah Kaufmann; she has such an amazing voice and I just loved the idea. We shot the video within a few hours, and it was so much fun. Shooting in the streets of NY, getting people involved. We didn't really plan much—it was mostly improv the whole day.

The video came out a few weeks later. The day after it came out, my phone was ringing off the hook from every news station. I couldn't believe it, because I seriously wasn't expecting it!

For the next few days it was a whirlwind experience, being on the news getting interviewed, I loved it!

All my life I knew exactly what I wanted to do, and I put my mind to it and I do it. I knew I wanted to model, act, and go to school to be a fashion designer. At 17 yrs old I moved to NY to attend FIT. While there I started modeling and acting. I loved it so much. I have been working hard ever since graduation. This video (Obama Girl) I feel was a great opportunity for me—it was the stepping stone I needed. I will continue pursuing acting and modeling after this video just as I did before. I have a lot of amazing things I am working on right now so it's very exciting. In the long run I see myself doing more film and eventually starting my clothing line, along with other business ventures.

A lot of people say "you're famous now." I laugh because I don't feel that way, I'm still the same person I was before.

Fame is hard for some people to handle. It can be a great thing and it can be a terrible thing. I have a wonderful family and I like balance in my life, so I'm just going to keep doing what I do.

★ 82

SECRET #20: THE DEATH OF THE E-ZINE

Before MySpace and Facebook, there was another form of online viral marketing that still can have value today. What the hell ever happened to e-zines, online newsletters that companies mailed directly to a list of subscribers? In the wake of social networking services, many buzz mongers have forgotten the power of email. Everyone checks email, usually at least once a day. A newsletter is an easy way to keep in contact with those who are interested in your cause and let them know the new information and products you are offering.

I run a newsletter with a significant number of subscribers. (If you want to join, send a blank email message to dseaman@gmail.com with "Subscribe" in the subject line.) I'll send out a quick "article" with some cool ideas and thoughts about once every two weeks or so. From time to time, I'll plug a website or product in these newsletters. When I do, traffic to the linked site *skyrockets* within a matter of hours—thousands of clicks will come in. So, clearly, the newsletter is still a fantastic buzz engine. Plus, people can hit "reply" and respond to your email, giving you feedback in real time.

I'd encourage you to set up an opt-in newsletter on one of the free services such as Google Groups (http://groups.google.com) or Topica (http://topica.com). Put a subscribe box on your website, and invite your friends and colleagues to join your newsletter. Please note that an opt-in newsletter is different from indiscriminately spamming people. "Opt-in" means that a person has to enter their email address on your site and then click on an additional confirmation link emailed to them before they will begin receiving your newsletters. This ensures that only those people who support your cause and are interested in buying your products actually join the list. Be aggressive in getting new people to join, however. Make sure you encourage people who visit your site to subscribe to your *free* newsletter—people have great difficulty resisting anything that's free. And you can list some of the specific topics you'll be covering in your newsletter to whet a potential subscriber's appetite. If you're running a financial tips newsletter, for example, a topic called "How I Made $250,000 Last Year While Sitting on My Couch" would get *me* to subscribe! Just keep it honest. Fantastical claims are easy to spot, especially online.

CHAPTER 5

When It Makes Sense to Pay for Attention: Teaming Up with the Godfather of the Internet

At a certain point, you may decide you want to jump-start your buzz campaign with some paid advertising. The benefits of paid traffic are numerous. For starters, visitors will be sent to your site within a matter of minutes. No waiting for days or weeks until a search engine appropriately indexes your site. Secondly, paid traffic can be rigidly targeted by region and audience—and you can write very specific ad copy so that only those truly interested in your product will click on the link. You can also use online advertising to direct thousands of visitors to your MySpace profile or blog.

SECRET #21: GOOGLE ADWORDS, AN OLDIE BUT A GOODIE

The granddaddy of online advertising services is Google AdWords. You can begin using the service with as little as $5 (and an additional $5 setup fee). You choose where your ads run, you choose the text for your ad and exactly where visitors are sent to, and you can view your statistics at any time. The advantage of AdWords over other systems is its reach: Google is the second-most-visited site on the Internet and also boasts an absolutely mammoth network of external sites displaying its text ads. To sign up, visit http://shutterline.com/adwords.html—I'll also be posting exclusive tips there for getting the most out of AdWords. I recommend spending around $75 to $150 to begin with; then pause your campaign and review your results. How many visitors did you receive? How many sales or leads resulted? Make sure your ad copy is specific. A site selling used books, for example, should put "Used Books" in the ad headline somewhere. Don't put something vague like "Everything is on sale!" because that will result in relatively untargeted traffic. Who knows if those clicks are people even *interested* in books? Since AdWords charges you by the click, the key is to make sure that every click counts. Unlike other forms of advertising, you don't need to create something that entices as many people as possible. You want an ad that will turn away anyone who is not a potential customer. Luckily, AdWords lets you change your ad text as many times as you want. Experiment with it.

And, for alternative advertising networks, which may charge you a flat rate per campaign (for example, $100 for a week-long ad on a popular political blog), you need to think differently. Since you're paying for an entire week of ad coverage, rather than only paying when a qualified visitor clicks on your link, the economics are fundamentally different. You paid $100 for seven days of coverage. Who *cares* if the visitors are incredibly targeted or not? You spent good money, and you want to get as many viewers as humanly possible to click on your ad. This drives down the final cost-per-click (CPC) of your campaign. CPC is calculated by dividing the total ad expenditure by the number of visitors the advertisement sent you.

With a flat-rate campaign, you want to create enticing ad copy. No question about it. One way of boosting your ad's attractiveness to viewers is to create a text headline that incorporates what I call "power words." These are words you hear constantly on television commercials: Free, easy, and safe, to name a few. These words are used relentlessly because they have a powerful psychological effect: Consumers *want* things to be safe and easy. If a company offers a product that's easy, then I know it won't take much of my time. I'll be more likely to click the ad and explore what is being offered. (My full explanation of power words can be found in Chapter 7.) I originally intended power words to be used subtly during radio interviews—however, I have discovered they are also immensely helpful in creating cost-effective advertisements.

The other simple way of boosting an ad's number of clicks is to create a "cliffhanger." Just as enticing headlines on news websites encourage you to click through for the full story, or as television networks give you a preview of what's to come after the commercial break, you can leave the visitor wanting more. Something as easy as leaving the second half of a sentence out of an advertisement will do the trick nicely. "Free for thirty days, plus you receive our…" Since text ads have a length limit anyway, visitors just assume you've been *accidentally* cut off. They click to find out what the heck you're offering them. This sounds pretty simple (it is), but trust me, it will have a significant impact on how well your ads perform. Advertisements that answer every single question in the reader's mind are not ads that receive clicks.

★ Smart Landing Pages

Your landing page is the page of your site where an advertisement sends visitors. **Quick secret: Your landing**

page should give the user *exactly* what they expected, or they will leave your site in a hurry without taking any action. An online coffee retailer, for example, should create a landing page with several photos of coffee beans, a steaming hot cup of fresh coffee, a man proudly serving an espresso, etc. This way the visitor is instantly drawn in. Large blocks of text are good for search engine positioning, but they will repel people clicking on your ad. The landing page should be colorful, contain relevant images, and engage the visitor directly. Any text should be large, and time-sensitive offers are particularly effective here. Perhaps you have a sale that ends on Friday: Mention this on the landing page! You want your visitor to feel as if what they are being offered *now* could be taken away at a future point—this is a major tenet of online marketing.

Landing pages are also referred to as "splash pages" by web designers for a reason: It should make a splash in the visitor's mind. Several striking images combined with a time-sensitive offer will engage the visitor. Three long paragraphs about the benefits of buying coffee from you, however, will just create boredom.

Your site should also contain a prominently featured link to a Frequently Asked Questions, or FAQ, page. This is simply a web page containing a list of questions you suspect potential customers might have ("Why should I buy my coffee from you versus at the grocery store?"; "Are any of your coffee beans organically grown?"; etc.) along with answers written by you.

The FAQ page is an excellent place to answer customer questions (and thus cut down on the number of unnecessary calls and email messages you receive), and it is also a great opportunity to convey your company's "personality"—answers can be spunky and informative to get visitors excited. The question about organic coffee, for example, is the perfect place to speak about your company's values and commitment to the environment.

Every landing page should have an easy method of contact: a toll-free phone number, a link to an email address, etc. You can also list a company-specific AOL screen name, if you have one, so that visitors can chat with you in real-time. If you don't have a screen name for your company, create one for free at http://aimexpress.aol.com. Experiment with the layout of your landing page until you find a design that "converts well"—in other words, a solid percentage of your visitors are making sales or inquiring about your product.

SECRET #22: BREAKDOWN OF OTHER ONLINE ADVERTISING SERVICES

Even though I strongly recommend you start with Google AdWords, your budget may be big enough that you want to experiment with several advertising networks at once. Here are some alternatives to Google:

Microsoft adCenter (http://adcenter.microsoft.com)

adCenter is basically Microsoft's answer to AdWords. The service is similar in most respects. When I've needed support, they have provided excellent and helpful customer service via phone. adCenter's commitment to quickly handling customer-support issues makes it a valuable alternative and worth trying.

Yahoo! Search Marketing (http://searchmarketing.yahoo.com)

Formerly called Overture, the new Yahoo! Search Marketing taps into Yahoo.com's considerable search-engine audience—and its large network of partner websites.

AdEngage (http://adengage.com)

Based in El Segundo, California, AdEngage is a privately owned advertising network describing itself as a "major online advertising network that displays ads on more than 2,500 websites and works with thousands of advertisers to display over ten billion ads every month." Results have been mixed—if you choose the right site to advertise on, the traffic can be amazing, but if not, it's not worth your time.

AdBrite (http://adbrite.com)

This is an advertising network with considerable clout, but customer-support options are woefully inadequate should something go wrong (no phone support for regular advertisers). As with AdEngage, if you advertise on the right property, the results can be substantial and well worth the price.

Etology (http://etology.com)

Yet another independently owned ad network with considerable inventory. Once you've bought a substantial amount from them, you'll be assigned your own account exec who can help you secure discounts for longer-running campaigns (generally thirty days or longer). Also provides phone support.

BlogAds (http://blogads.com)

BlogAds allows you to purchase ads "by the hive" (on a group of similar sites at once) or "a la carte" (where you choose the specific site where your ad will run). BlogAds is the advertising broker for many high-profile blogs, such as gossip site PerezHilton.com, and the packages tend to be expensive. Use selectively if your ad budget is large. Also, if your own blog starts to receive significant traffic (above ten thousand visitors per day), consider signing up as a publisher—you can make good money with this high-end niche network. Some blogs are pulling in over $5,000 a month from the service.

★ 92

SECRET #23: MAKING NICE WITH THE GODFATHER OF THE INTERNET

BUT, NOW YOU COME TO ME AND YOU SAY "DON CORLEONE, GIVE ME JUSTICE." BUT YOU DON'T ASK WITH RESPECT. YOU DON'T OFFER FRIENDSHIP. YOU DON'T EVEN THINK TO CALL ME GODFATHER.

—*Don Corleone*, The Godfather

Have you ever seen *The Godfather?* (The original, not Part II or III, although those should also be considered mandatory viewing.) Much as Don Corleone holds tremendous power—and rewards respect—search-giant Google can shower you with buzz riches beyond your wildest dreams. But you have to play by its rules.

Despite all the excitement surrounding social networking sites and bookmarking services, the fact remains that Google is the most powerful player in the search market. Learn how to position your website well, and the flood of highly targeted traffic may overwhelm you!

First of all: How does Google decide which results are shown first? How does it determine which sites end up receiving the vast majority of traffic? While some website owners speculate that Google's algorithm (its program for determining how to "rank" search results) contains as many as one hundred variables, there are really only two big ones: (1) Relative Popularity and (2) Frequency. If you're scratching your head, that's okay. We'll go over exactly what these two variables mean—and how to ethically maximize both. This will give your site the greatest chance of receiving favorable listings on Google. Before we continue, a quick warning: Google is smart. You should never attempt to "game" the system by loading up on irrelevant keywords. This can result in a permanent ban from their search results. Instead, focus on keywords that match your site's content. The key to good listings is, above all else, having great content on your pages. Solid content—especially with a heavy emphasis on text—makes the rest of this process easy.

Relative Popularity, as I call it, is the number of other websites on the Internet that link to your site. This makes sense: Google assumes that if hundreds or thousands of other people are linking to your web page, you must have something of value. Now, it's a little more sophisticated than that, because Google uses a system called PageRank to determine the relative "credibility" of a site linking to yours. What do I mean? Let's say you launch your website and then tell all of your friends to link to it, in hopes of boosting your search-engine ranking. Your friends dutifully do this (they're good friends!), and soon you have close to a hundred links pointed to your site. Chances are, most of these links are on personal pages and small-time blogs. This doesn't impress Google's system, because the sites linking to yours have a relatively low PageRank—in other words, Google knows they aren't that "influential" on the Internet. Don't get me wrong: Links to your site will help you. But the *quality* of the sites linking to yours is far more important than the sheer number. Let's say that instead of having a hundred friends link to your new site, you get a quote in a popular regional newspaper such as the *Chicago Tribune* or *Baltimore Sun*. On the newspaper's website, the article links to your page. Google's bot (an automated program that sifts through billions of web pages for new content) notices the link to your site—and Google knows that the *Chicago Tribune* is an influential publication with a lot of pageviews a day, as well as a real-world audience. The newspaper's PageRank is, therefore, relatively high. Its PageRank is partially "transmitted" to your site: Now you suddenly have a higher PageRank within Google's system. You've rubbed shoulders with a popular website, and a fraction of that popularity rubs off onto your site.

I know this sounds weird, but it's crucial to understand. A link to your site on, say, CNN.com or BBC.co.uk (both with presumably very high PageRank scores) would automatically boost your site's visibility within Google's search results. The search engine assumes your site must be valuable if CNN or the BBC is linking to it. Don't despair if you have no idea how to get a link on either of those sites—there's a handy trick for boosting your Relative Popularity, and I'll share it with you in a minute. First, we need to go over the second major variable that influences your ranking on Google. I keep saying "Google," but the techniques here will also significantly improve your ranking on the other major engines—Yahoo! Search and Microsoft Live (formerly known as MSN Search). Even though their algorithms are different, they still care about Relative Popularity and Frequency.

Frequency is the number of times certain keywords appear on your page. The size and placement of text may also affect how your keyword frequency is perceived by the search engine. For example, if you are a real estate broker in Manhattan, you would want the words "Manhattan Real Estate" in relatively large text toward the top of your page. You wouldn't want this crucial phrase to be only in tiny text at the bottom. You'd also want that phrase, and others like it ("New York apartments" for example), to appear within the text of your page. Your site's title should include several of your most important search phrases. In this case, "Manhattan Real Estate—New York apartments, sublets, and brownstones" would work as an excellent title. "David Seaman | Realtor" (if I were a realtor, which I'm not!) would be, on the other hand, a title that is *not* search-engine friendly. It gives the search engine's bot no clue as to what the page is actually about.

You may have seen sites that try to overdo their keyword frequency. Continuing with the real estate website example, the welcome text would read: "Welcome to my Manhattan real estate homepage—we offer tons of different apartments in New York, sublets in New York, New York apartments, New York leases, residential offerings, one-bedroom, two-bedroom, pre-war, affordable pre-war apartments, and much more. Manhattan real estate is very competitive, and we appreciate you visiting our site for all of your Manhattan real estate and New York apartment needs!" The website owner is obviously trying to show up in search results for things like "New York apartment," but in the process he has created a website that makes *no sense whatsoever* to human readers. It sounds like the ramblings of an insane person, and I would be wary of trusting such a broker with my business. Also, the search engine bot won't buy this—anecdotal evidence suggests that loading your page with too many repetitive keywords is actually bad for your ranking. The search engine is in the business of providing users with good results. It doesn't want to send visitors to pages that are little more than nonsensical phrases repeated over and over again.

If your title contains the appropriate keywords for your business, and these keywords are repeated three or four times within the text of your web page, this is more than enough. The search engine bot will "understand" what your page is about and rank it accordingly.

THE ENERGY-SAVING SEARCH ENGINE?

Visit Blackle.com sometime, and what you find will surprise you: A search engine almost identical to Google (it is powered by Google's Custom Search, in fact) with one crucial distinction. The background is black. This rethinking of the typical white-background, search-engine site is significantly easier on the eyes, but Blackle's founders don't care about that. They wanted to create a search engine that would be more "environmentally friendly"—black background web pages typically require less energy from your computer's monitor. The site claims to have saved a whopping 383,294 Watt hours of power thus far.

SECRET #24: GOOGLE JUICE: LINKS FROM HIGHLY RATED SITES

One obvious way to boost your PageRank, and thus increase your odds of favorable listings on Google, is to get links from highly rated sites. While Google frowns upon purchasing links for this sole purpose—and may even penalize sites that sell such links—there is no rule against creating links on content-driven sites. If you have a MySpace page, *definitely* link to your external website. Also, go to a site called Squidoo.com, and create a "lens" with a link to your site. Originally developed by marketing guru Seth Godin, Squidoo allows users to create a topic-specific article (or "lens" as they call it) complete with a few paragraphs of insight and links to appropriate websites.

So, if I were a real estate agent in New York, I would write two or three paragraphs about how competitive getting an apartment in the city can be, and then include a link to my website—and maybe a link to a few competitors' sites as well, so that I don't seem like a total hack. Squidoo is popular and ranks well on the search engines; it has what one user on their site refers to as "Google juice." While the evidence is anecdotal, I've definitely noticed a boost in traffic from Google searches within a few days of creating new Squidoo pages. So it is worth doing as a part of your overall positioning efforts. You can also post links on these websites, in the hopes of increasing your search-engine profile:

Propeller.com

Owned by Time Warner and a service of AOL, Propeller is a high-profile link-sharing website similar in structure to Reddit and Digg. You can also get a nice initial traffic boost from the link itself. As with all link-sharing websites, only submit your best content, and don't abuse the system by repeatedly self-promoting. One or two links is more than enough.

Furl.net

Yet another link-sharing website, Furl is worth submitting to from time to time.

StumbleUpon.com

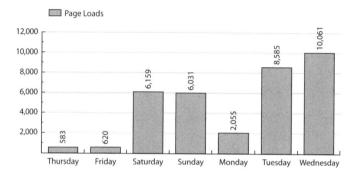

□ Page Loads

The StumbleUpon Effect: **I posted an article to one of my websites as a test for this section. Notice how during the first two days, it only receives around 1,200 views. This traffic is mostly from search engines and bookmarking sites. Then on Saturday a submission to StumbleUpon starts to pay off— 6,159 views. The figure drops significantly on Monday (New Year's Eve; many people were out partying and away from their computers) and then regains on Tuesday. By Wednesday, my article is receiving over 10,000 views per 24 hours.**

With over four million active users, StumbleUpon is worth taking seriously. The site has users download a small toolbar, which attaches itself to a web browser such as Internet Explorer or Firefox. Then it allows users to "thumbs up" or "thumbs down" any website they view. The sites with consistently high ratings are shown to other users. Here's how the service describes itself: "StumbleUpon uses ratings to form collaborative opinions on website quality. When you stumble, you will only see pages which friends and like-minded stumblers have recommended. This helps you discover great content you probably wouldn't find using a search engine."

When you first join, and sporadically thereafter, the service asks what kinds of content you're interested in (sports, tech news, photography, self-improvement, astronomy, etc.) so it can display sites that you are likely to find useful.

However, you only want to submit your own content from time to time. Use the service heavily for a few days before submitting anything—some users speculate that this can increase your "influence" within the network. Then, once you submit your site, the recommendation will be taken seriously and shown to other StumbleUpon users. If it is good content, a certain percentage of these users will give your page a quick "thumbs up," which in turn guarantees it will be shown to an even wider pool of users. This can all happen very quickly: When I submit a high-quality article posted to one of my websites, it's not unusual to receive ten thousand or more new visitors in a twenty-four-hour period just from StumbleUpon. And highly rated content can continue to be shown for several weeks.

The inner workings of precisely how the system operates are not known; the company keeps this sort of information private for competitive reasons. Still, it has an uncanny ability to deliver intriguing new content to users, based on their interests and past voting behavior. The key to success with StumbleUpon is easy to remember: Great content. Nothing else will convince users to "thumbs up" your site.

SECRET #25: BUILDING A WEBSITE AND UNLOCKING GOOGLE'S SECRETS

I've already shown you how to maximize your chances of a solid Google listing. Of course, all of this depends on having a good website in the first place. If you don't have one, how do you set one up?

First of all, I recommend you get a memorable domain name (your-name.com, for example)—this costs around $10 per year, but the fee is frequently waived if you purchase a new web-hosting account. "Web hosting" is simply a service that physically hosts your website files. When a visitor types in my site address, for example, the web page is loaded from a server owned by Yahoo! in California. I pay Yahoo! Web Hosting on a monthly basis for this service. I've been with many different web-hosting companies over the years, and I've found Yahoo! Web Hosting (http://webhosting.yahoo.com) to be the best in terms of reliability and price. Should you have any questions, they also have toll-free phone support, which is a serious selling point. You can't imagine how frustrating it is to experience website downtime, especially during a TV appearance or ad campaign, and not have anyone there to help you fix it in real time. Plans start at $11.95 per month.

Also, the account control panel is packed with features and includes many pre-designed templates. All you have to do is fill in the appropriate text boxes and hit "Publish!"—this is especially helpful for those unfamiliar with HTML (one of the major programming languages used to design web pages).

If you want a free web host, consider Google Pages (http://www.googlepages.com) or the excellently designed Tumblr (http://www.tumblr.com). Both services have a wide variety of designs to choose from, and Tumblr allows you to create a professional-looking blog in about five minutes.

You want your content to be text-based to maximize your odds of a good Google placement. Avoid image-only pages or web pages based on Flash animations. Text is the easiest kind of page to create, and it's "search-engine friendly"—avoid fancy designs that impress but don't contain much in the way of actual information. Search engines won't know how to classify them and therefore can't direct people to them.

If you want to create top-notch web pages, but want more flexibility than a template can provide, consider using Microsoft FrontPage. This software program, available at any computer store, allows you to create well-designed websites with about as little hassle as creating a Microsoft Word document. To create truly great web pages from scratch, however, you'll need to learn HTML. Take a course at the local university, or pick up one of the numerous books on HTML design available in bookstores. As far as programming languages go, it's fairly easy to learn.

When you design your site, only provide relevant information and make contacting you easy. FrontPage allows you to create a sophisticated "contact us" web form with only a few clicks; Yahoo! Web Hosting shows you how to include this useful feature on your site as well.

Avoid providing numerous links to other websites or competitors without good reason—people will simply click on the links and leave your site. Also, linking to dozens of unrelated websites can hurt your search engine standing. Only link to information and external websites that will be potentially useful to your visitors.

★ Tracking Services

Wonder how many visitors per day your site gets? Or where they're coming from? Put a free web tracker on your site. These services will provide you with real-time updates on who is visiting your website. A good web tracker will provide the following information, and possibly more:

- **Referring URL.** This is the website a visitor was viewing immediately before checking out your site— this way you can tell where your traffic is coming from.
- **Recent search terms.** Which keywords are people using to find you on Google and the other search

engines? Which search engines are sending you the most traffic?

- **Visit length and visitor paths.** A "visit length" is simply how long someone views your website, while a visitor path shows each web page within your site that a visitor has checked out—and in which order they were viewed. (Example: A visitor may first view my welcome page, then my bio/background page, then my contact information page, and then leave the site.)

- **Operating system and browser.** Most web trackers will tell you which operating system (such as Windows XP, Windows Vista, Macintosh OS X, Linux, etc.) your visitor's computer has, in addition to which web browser was used when viewing your site (Microsoft Internet Explorer or Mozilla Firefox, for example). This information is useless for the vast majority of basic website owners, but it can be helpful when analyzing visitor behavior. For example, if you notice a disproportionate number of visitors using Windows Mobile, then you know that visitors (for whatever reason) prefer to view your site from their mobile phones when they are away from home or the office.

- **ISP and geographic location.** You'll see the city and country where each visitor is located, in addition to their Internet service provider (in most instances). So a visitor located in Charlotte, North Carolina, with aol.com as the ISP is likely an America Online subscriber who lives in Charlotte. A visitor located in

New York, New York, with hearst.com as the ISP is likely an employee of Hearst Magazines surfing your site from work, while a visitor with reshall.nyu.edu as the ISP is a NYU student viewing your site from a residence hall Internet connection.

My favorite free web trackers are **StatCounter.com** and **SiteMeter.com**. Signing up for either service is easy, and they both include instructions for installing the tracker on your website. **Google Analytics** (http://www.google.com/analytics/) is another free, reliable tracking service worth checking out.

CHAPTER 6

How to Get on Television

Let's face it: You aren't the first person who wants to be on Oprah's couch. You're not the first buzz-hungry whore to lust over an interview with Matt Lauer, Anderson Cooper, or a wild-eyed Bill O'Reilly. There are millions of people clamoring for buzz. Unless you're already a Kathy Griffin, an Al Gore, or a Paris Hilton, getting national TV bookers to take an interest in you can be a challenge. Luckily, there's a way in. It's very simple. Are you ready for it?

SECRET #26: TV DOESN'T MAKE YOU—YOU MAKE YOU

Here are some very simple words that will help get you on TV: **Create the buzz yourself.** Don't rely on any TV show to "make you," for an Oprah Winfrey or Jay Leno or Jon Stewart to pluck your ass out of obscurity. The only way to make yourself valuable to any show is to have something going on. Do everything in your power to build a little online empire—post and share viral videos and other absurd media creations (more on this in Chapter 10). The Internet is the best way to hit buzz gold, and when that happens, things will take off *very* quickly. You don't need to get on every TV show—you only need to get on *one* popular one. From there, you'll be written about in newspapers and on blogs, and asked to appear as a guest on smaller shows. Radio producers will try to get you on their programs as well for a few sound bites. Accept as many offers to be on-air as is reasonably possible.

What do all of these nouveau famous have in common? More often than not, there's something a little *crazy* about them. The average person doesn't spend her time defending Britney Spears, crafting a civil rights protest in support of Paris Hilton, or flitting around in a bikini singing about how much she loves Barack Obama. The average person doesn't strum a guitar in Times Square wearing only underwear. Your campaign needs to be bold enough for people to *want* to spread the word. Because it's funny or weird or just different from all of the other mediocre garbage in our media universe.

So the secret here would have to be: Do what others aren't willing to do, either because they aren't crazy or savvy enough. The rising class of Internet and reality TV stars usually have a tenuous grasp on reality, or, at the very least, the ability to spice things up. For many people, watching an outrageous four-minute video on YouTube may be the highlight of their entire day. People are cubicle slaves, more bored than ever before, and this creates an opportunity. New stars are being made every day. New companies are getting their products recognized by trying absolutely batshit-crazy publicity stunts.

Just look at how bizarre television commercials have become in the past few years. A soda commercial, an advertisement for a simple carbonated sugary beverage, is now often a surreal and shocking freakshow. I recently saw a car commercial for Scion, Toyota's youth-targeted line of automobiles, in which cartoon monsters literally *eat* people. Not a single mention of the car's performance or features; just the crazy shock value. Nowadays, people are compelled by the outrageous, and knowing this can make you a star.

SECRET #27: TV SHOW JEALOUSY

If you go to the junior prom with an unbelievably attractive date from a rival school, people take note of it. Even if you were previously known only as the guy with a one-sixteenth-size replica of the Millennium Falcon in his bedroom, your image will shift. Come Monday morning classes, the girls in your grade will look at you in an entirely different light. Sure, you might have a thing for *Star Wars* memorabilia, but you can also land a hot date.

The point here is that perceptions *can* be changed—and often quickly. Although this book focuses on building dynamic buzz—getting TV producers to approach you, and not vice versa!—you may have a few email addresses of producers who have shot down your pitches in the past. If you don't, I'll show you how to get them. If you do, keep these addresses handy, and when lightning strikes—you get invited onto a national TV or radio show—send out a quick blast to your most important contacts.

A couple of pointers here: If you have less than ten contacts, just send out the email messages individually. If you *must*, send out a generic message to all of them, but *make sure* you put their addresses in the blind copy field, or build an email list that doesn't allow them to see who else you're contacting. It's totally obnoxious when someone sends you a pitch, and you can see who else has been sent the exact same pitch. Some people don't even consider ideas that have been submitted to other people as well.

If you learn only one thing from this chapter, it is this: Blind copy everything.

Your email should be brief and to the point; producers and on-air talent are often very busy. The subject line can simply be their name and the name of the network they work for—this guarantees that it will be read and not accidentally marked as spam. It is acceptable for your email to simply state the facts: "On NBC *Today Show* tomorrow 5/1, available for additional interviews," followed by your phone number and other contact information. It also implies that you don't have the time to hammer out an overly self-congratulatory email. And it's purely business— your story has become hot and you're offering that hotness to other shows!

You may want to consider buying a BlackBerry or similar mobile Internet device, if you don't yet have one, to keep in constant touch with your email, MySpace page, etc. Many cable news shows decide the day's stories in the morning, and there can be last-minute changes or a decision to invite you on. You might miss out on this email if you don't have wireless email access. (I personally own an iPhone, which has full Internet access and is slimmer than most BlackBerry devices.)

The secret here is to *always* remain accessible. Unless your name is Brad Pitt, inaccessibility can only work against you. Especially when you first start out, producers and bookers will expect you to be easy to work with. If you're too much trouble to lock down, they *will* find somebody else. (Later in the game, it's okay to appear in demand, but that is *entirely* different from being inaccessible. And ideally your future unavailability is not feigned—it is due to the fact that you're genuinely too busy with other media requests!)

SECRET #28: HANDLING YOUR FIRST CALL FROM A TV BOOKER

Your first call or email from a TV booker will come after you've established some degree of local or online buzz. The email will be impossible to miss: "Interview request" or something similar will be the subject line. It will be a brief but polite request for you to call someone and confirm your availability to do the show.

These requests come with the built-in assumption that *of course* you want to be on TV. And you do! Don't act like a diva or make scheduling you overly difficult: It's not as if the show won't go on without you. In many cases, the guest lineup is finalized only a few hours before the show starts, so definitely respond as soon as you can.

Your phone call will usually consist of something called a "pre-interview," where a producer will basically ask for your stance on different topics of interest to the show. While there's no right or wrong answer in most cases, just don't play it safe; don't go with "I don't know" or "I don't think it really matters either way." If you're being asked to appear on a show, they want you to be enthusiastic and *opinionated.* Let your energy come across over the phone; get excited and convey that excitement to the producer. After all, in a matter of hours, a couple million people will know about your cause or brand. It's worth getting a little worked up over.

I remember auditioning in person for a pilot at MTV. The casting director called me back about a week later after having reviewed the answers I'd given on camera. He said I was great, but there wasn't enough energy. So I came back in, and we taped the interview again, and this time I was brimming with enthusiasm. Most people aren't given a second chance—if you're lethargic, you just aren't going to land shows!

SECRET #29: WHAT TO EXPECT: GREEN ROOM, MAKEUP, PISS IN YOUR PANTS

At most shows, you'll check in with security at the front desk and provide some form of ID. A producer should already have you listed on the guest sheet, so this process should be painless. When the security guard asks for your ID, don't be like, "I'm on the show. Don't you *know* who I am?" There's no reason to be obnoxious about it, and chances are the guard has met people a lot more famous than you anyway.

Once you have a temporary ID badge, you'll go up to whatever floor the show is on. In many cases a staffer will lead you there so you don't get lost. You'll head to the green room, which isn't nearly as exciting as the *Jimmy Kimmel Live* green room depicted on *Entourage*. For many TV shows, it can be just a simple room with a screen showing whatever program is currently on-air. Your few minutes in the green room are a time to prepare, look over your notes one last time, and get yourself pumped up. You don't have to worry about stage fright: Most TV interviews feel personal since it's just you, a few guests, and the host. You don't "notice" the fact that millions of people are watching in their homes.

Also while in the green room, you can briefly chat with the other guests. They'll probably be reviewing their notes also. If the topic being discussed is controversial, you can be sneaky and try to build alliances with them. Don't say to another guest, "Just agree with me on the show, okay?" Find out where other guests stand on the main issues and tell them areas where you both agree. When a fellow guest says you're right on the money during your interview, this makes you seem credible to viewers.

From the green room, you'll be ushered in for a quick makeup session. Some shows will apply makeup the old-fashioned way, while others use a spray gun to quickly apply it. You'll look like an orange freak by the time they're done, but this is good, because you'll look absolutely great on camera. **Here's a fun secret: Don't recoil when they use the spray gun or apply makeup near your eyes. This is something "first-timers" do, and makeup artists can tell who is new to TV from this reaction alone.** It doesn't really matter, but it's fun to pretend you're a pro! And the makeup artists *know* not to get any in your eyes, so don't bother reminding them. They may or may not apply a special lip gloss so your lips don't reflect too much light during the interview.

After makeup, the interview will begin. If the host and guests are physically right near you, you can just hold a normal conversation. Be expressive with your face, and share your ideas with conviction. If you're on a camera feed by yourself, or if you're doing the show via satellite, you should look into the camera lens the entire time. Even when you don't think you're being asked a question, shows will sometimes do a split-screen reaction shot to see what the other guests feel about a particular comment made on the show. If you're in front of the camera, you're potentially on-air. Keep this in mind.

Always look into the camera lens, never into the monitor below it! Many shows will have a live feed of the show on a screen directly beneath the camera, so you can follow along. This is fine to check occasionally, but when you're answering a question, say it into the camera—just ignore the screen. It will distract you. Some shows don't have a monitor for you to check, which often results in a better interview—you're more focused on the quality of your answers. And those answers should be intelligent but *quick.* You're not writing a paper.

You'll have an earpiece so that you can hear the show's audio and any comments from the control room during a commercial break. For example, if you're slouching to one side or not making eye contact with the camera, control will mention this to you during a break.

This sounds kind of complex, but it's really easy. You're just talking into a piece of glass in front of you. Talking into a camera lens is actually *easier* than any other kind of conversation, because you don't have to make eye contact with another person. So it feels natural to stare ahead the entire time. This looks great to viewers; they get the feeling that you're making confident eye contact with them.

Many shows will encourage you to "jump in" if a guest says something you disagree with; feel free to do this! "I completely disagree, Ann," you could say, and then the host will ask why you disagree. Now's your chance to shine and really lay down your major points. Plus it gets you more camera time, and viewers will be more likely to remember whatever it is you're promoting.

While you're on the show, the control room will be sporadically flashing your name and plugging whatever cause, book, or website you've asked them to key in. You're essentially advertising on television for free!

SECRET #30: TURNING ONE SHOW INTO FIFTEEN SHOWS

As mentioned, once you're booked on a show, send out an email "blast" to a few other producers. Keep your message brief; just tell them what show you'll be on, what you'll be talking about, and when they can watch it. Everybody wants a "hot" guest, especially if your area of expertise is in high demand for a certain story in the news. Close your message with a phone number they can reach you at; phone contact is more immediate than a bunch of email messages back and forth. And remember the rules we discussed before—always, always blind copy if you're sending an email message to more than one producer.

If you don't have any producers' email addresses, just send to the "generic" show address advertised on a particular program's website. These emails eventually *do* get read by someone, and if your topic is a high priority, it will be forwarded to a booker or producer.

Don't limit yourself to television producers. If you're on a TV show, radio producers will most likely love to book you. Radio shows work on very short schedules and are often very inviting. There's no doubt about it: Radio is easier to get on. Build on the momentum of a TV appearance by going on a bunch of radio talk shows. It may not feel as glamorous to you, but radio can have just as much of an impact as TV bookings, if not more. Listeners are attached to certain shows and hosts. Appearing on the air while someone is listening in their car, tired and returning home from a long day's work, is an intimate experience. You have the potential to touch a lot of people with your message or hook.

And radio shows are easy to do; most of the time you can just do a phone-in interview at an agreed-upon time. It's a five- or ten-minute phone conversation; then you hang up the telephone and realize that close to a million listeners now know who you are! This lack of prep time means you can do a ton of interviews in a single day. Television takes much longer, because you have to factor in extra time to get to the studio and get yourself camera ready, and most producers want you to show up plenty early in case there are any unforeseen issues.

★ Keep Getting Booked

Getting asked back to TV shows or parlaying one appearance into twenty comes down to one thing: Knowing the show and presenting well. Broadcast journalism programs are littered with good-looking people who can assemble a sentence on the fly. That's not enough: You need to know the show you're on. If you can, watch other guests a couple nights beforehand. Get a feel for the host's style and the pace of the show. Figure out when exactly you'll want to plug your cause—and how to do this without interrupting the flow.

Buzz on the national level is both a crapshoot and an art form. In all likelihood, you aren't going to get booked every week. For most entrepreneurs and aspiring buzz mongers, just one or two national mentions a *year* would be considered excellent. This is why you need to have more immediate forms of buzz: A Facebook platform, a MySpace presence, a rapidly growing opt-in newsletter system. You need to keep your name or your product on the tip of everyone's tongue, even if you're *not* landing any big shows. We'll talk more about this later.

WHY CNN LIKES BILL MAHER

Flip to CNN and you're likely to see Bill Maher; he's a guest on *Larry King Live* and *The Situation Room* all the time. If you wanted to be cynical, you could say he gets booked so often because Time Warner (CNN's parent company) also owns HBO, where Maher hosts his weekly talk show. I'm sure that doesn't hurt anything, but it's not the real reason he gets so much airtime. *He's a damn good guest.* When Bill Maher is on, regardless of the topic at hand, the host and producers are certain he'll come up with something witty. He is quick on his feet and isn't at all afraid to say controversial things on the air—and then back them up. Hell, he's been fired from on-air positions for saying things that management didn't agree with. Maher will sneak in with a joke or two and then cut down a politician or a policy. Viewers at home are nodding their heads in agreement: He says what we want to say, only more eloquently. And he uses the power of humor. Jon Stewart does the same thing.

Better still, those who despise him (conservatives, mostly) tune in, curious to see what he'll say this time. This builds buzz for any show he's on and ensures that he gets invited back. Shows want viewers above all else. **The secret to learn from Bill Maher is this: Hold nothing back.** Speak your mind, don't dumb it down. Get passionate, and by all means, don't worry about pissing people off. A guest who pleases one hundred percent of viewers is a terrible guest.

If you want a role model for having balls on the air, Bill Maher is perfect. He was doing his live weekly show, *Real Time With Bill Maher,* when hecklers started shouting about how 9/11 was a conspiracy. One held up a sign that read, "9/11 is a cover-up fraud."

119 ★

Maher had a heavy-hitting guest lineup that evening, including MSNBC's Chris Matthews, so he was not at all thrilled about a couple of people ruining his show on live national television. As the Associated Press later quoted him as saying, Maher yelled at his heckler, "Do we have some (expletive) security in this building, or do I have to come down there and kick his (expletive)?"

Maher ran off the stage and literally pushed the heckler out of his building, yelling, "Out! Out! Out!" Then he reminded his audience that they weren't there to verbally participate in the show: "Audience comes from the Latin, meaning 'to listen.'"

It was a brilliant handling of an awkward situation, and other members of the audience later told the Associated Press that it was some of the most exciting television they had ever seen!

★ 120

SECRET #31: GET YOUR MESSAGE ACROSS, NO MATTER WHAT

You only live once. And, more to the point, your window of opportunity for national buzz may be limited. Assume every show you're on is your last. Pick your three major points, things you want every person in America to know about, and drive those home with passion and zeal.

Also, keep in mind that television and radio interviews are not academic discussions! You don't need to present a bibliography or be otherwise boring—but you should do some research before the show starts. Have facts on hand that illuminate your point well and that will naturally impress the audience. For example, if your company markets a product to bored frequent flyers, you could say, "There are, on average, 61,000 people airborne above the United States at any given hour during the day. Our product appeals to these travelers by . . . " That's a stunning fact that will stick in viewers' minds.

Your notes, if you bring any with you to the studio, should just be short little sound bites and bulleted points you plan on mentioning while on-air. No paragraphs of information; you don't want to be reading something off a sheet of paper. Most hosts are so good at their jobs that you won't even realize fifteen, thirty, or forty-five minutes have passed by; they'll focus their questions, and the interview will *naturally* progress.

★ Media Guts

If you're on the radio or television, you can't curse (unless it's HBO), but you can say *just about anything else.* Be opinionated and stick to your opinions if you want to be invited back on shows, and if you want to get your message across in a memorable way. You aren't really on the air to have an intelligent discussion. You don't need to let the host "win you over" to their side. You are there to provide *opposition,* to create some on-air tension. Don't be afraid to shake your head and speak your mind.

Have conviction and express it. Even if you land a major media appearance, this won't convert into sales or interest unless you are someone viewers remember.

Wear clothes to the studio that display respect for the show and make you feel good about yourself—even if it's a radio interview! You'd be surprised how much of an impact clothing can have on your psyche. When you're in the studio wearing a Hugo Boss button-down and black pants, you'll *feel* like a real media personality. If you're wearing a T-shirt and look like you just rolled out of bed, you won't be able to tap into that same confidence!

Self-doubt has absolutely no place in a publicity whore's life! Confidence is a mediagenic quality that will take you far. I'm not saying you need to spend all of your money on Tony Robbins motivational tapes, but I *am* saying you need to have some conviction to pull off a great interview. More on this later.

★ 122

One secret to keep in mind: You look and sound much better than you realize. TV makeup gives your face a youthful glow and cancels out most blemishes. You'll look like someone *born* to be on television. And simply by virtue of being a guest on a radio show, listeners give you a tremendous amount of credit—they naturally assume you have something meaningful to share, or you wouldn't have been invited on in the first place. Act like you know you're doing well, because you are.

SECRET #32: THE AFTER-BUZZ: YOUTUBE YOUR APPEARANCES!

Find a friend who is TiVo-savvy, and have them record your television appearances. Better yet, some shows will even give you a recorded DVD of the interview segment if you ask nicely for it. You can also purchase archived show

DVDs from the network itself, usually somewhere on their website in the transcripts section.

Put a few seconds, and by this I mean not an entire ten-minute interview, on YouTube, Vimeo, and whatever other vide-sharing sites you frequent. Send out a newsletter blast to your loyal fans with a link to the video: Encourage them to share it with friends. You can also send a group message on Facebook or MySpace with the link.

Also, here's a secret: Post a link to your YouTube clip on all of the major bookmarking sites. Add it to Reddit.com, StumbleUpon.com, Del.icio.us, Digg.com, and Furl.net. This is a great way to quickly ignite discussion and promote viral spread of your clip.

SECRET #33: TO THANK OR NOT TO THANK

Showing Gratitude to Bookers

When you land a great national radio or TV guest spot, obviously send a thank-you email to the booker after the show. Tell them you had fun and received a lot of positive comments from fans after appearing on the show. But don't feel any obligation to go beyond that.

You don't have to send wine or a gift basket or anything crazy. Booking relevant guests is a booker's job. The best "gift" you can give them is a stellar on-air performance—it makes them look good when the guests they invite on are knowledgeable and witty.

Save the booker's email address and phone number. A few months after your interview, touch base with him—send a short email message to remind him of who you are, ask if he is still a booker at the same show, and briefly update him on any new projects you're doing. He may feel that your new project or cause fits in well with an upcoming show topic. So definitely stay in touch with your contacts, but don't seem overeager. That's why I suggest only touching base every couple months, as opposed to every few weeks. Bookers want to feel that you're a sought-after expert in your area. They aren't interested in people who will do anything to get booked. This is something that took me a little while to realize: Stay true to yourself. Buzz for the sake of buzz isn't all that exciting—what's exciting is buzz in pursuit of *something*, whether it be to sell a book you've written, plug a new website you're involved with, or to raise money for a promising new charity.

SECRET #34: THE MINIMAL—YET REAL—THREAT OF STALKERS

It's worth noting that many celebrities regularly get threats from viewers. Even I received threatening email after a particular television appearance. This is sadly a part of life for the buzz whore. It's unpleasant, to say the least, but I remind myself that in most cases, harassment does not lead to anything serious. It's some bored guy in his basement firing off an email message because he's unhappy with his own life: He doesn't *actually* plan on coming to New York and kicking my ass. Still, it's creepy all the same, and it's a part of life for anyone who continually whips up buzz.

Late-night talk show host Conan O'Brien was recently in the papers for having a self-described "priest-stalker" who has been sending him bizarre letters and following him around the world. According to one article, the deranged priest sent him a card postmarked from the same Italian town Conan was vacationing in at the time. Beyond creepy.

If you get idle threats after appearing on a national television show, keep it in perspective. How likely is it that Sue from Lansing, Michigan, is going to pull a *Single White Female* on you? Not very. With that said, there are some deranged people in this country, so if a letter or email message specifically threatens your life, forward it to law enforcement. Send it to your local police and the police in the recipient's jurisdiction. You can also visit the government's cybercrime task force website at http://www.ic3.gov for more contacts. IC3 will route your complaint to online crime divisions at the local, state, and national levels.

Despite the risks of being in the public eye, I personally feel it's worth it. Some people may not be willing to sacrifice *any* degree of safety for notoriety. I can understand that. But keep in mind that we live in a society where even "anonymity" does not protect you. If you own a MySpace page or a public website, you're potentially opening yourself up to harassment. Don't freak out, but at the same time remember to keep authorities informed—chances are, if someone is bothering *you*, they are bothering other people as well.

Overall, buzz whoring is rewarding and fun. You're contributing to the national dialogue; you're creating greater visibility for your organization; you're making people's mundane lives a little brighter. Don't let a handful of weirdos interrupt your creative flow. The worst thing you can do is to stop appearing on TV or to take down your website. Do you think Conan O'Brien plans on giving up his lucrative late-night talk show just because of a single demented man of the cloth? I don't think so!

SECRET #35: WHAT TELEVISION PRODUCERS REALLY THINK

I asked MSNBC senior producer and on-air personality Willie Geist to comment on the sort of celebrity culture this book explores—and to provide some insight into what sort of story would interest a producer. This is his intriguing answer.

★ 126

I think one of the main reasons celebrity news is so popular is because stories about movie stars are easy. By that I mean the story asks absolutely nothing of you. You flip on the TV, you see Paris Hilton being hauled away from her house crying in the back of a police car, and the facts of the story are of no consequence. I'll give you a hundred dollars if you can tell me the crime that sent Paris to jail. It's just a recognizable face whose life story you may have been following in a very general way and it's vaguely amusing that she's in an uncomfortable position.

Real news, on the other hand, is not so easy. To follow a story about Iraq closely, you have to have some understanding of who is involved in the war, of the complicated place where the war is being fought, and of why we're fighting the war. A hard news story requires you to consider a lot of information and to arrive at some opinion about it. That's not an easy thing to do. Paris Hilton, on the other hand, IS an easy thing to do.

Put it this way: it's a lot more fun to go to a Will Ferrell movie where you just sit back and let him go streaking through the quad than to go to a complex, "important" movie that teaches us lessons about the times we live in. I guess what I'm getting at is: people hate to think.

Admittedly, there is an element of ghoulishness to celebrity news. Our fascination with Britney Spears losing her kids or Lindsay Lohan going to rehab probably says something about us that we don't want to think about too deeply. The perception is that celebrity's lives are unfairly easy, so we take some perverse pleasure when they are brought back down to Earth. When they resemble us more closely.

These celebrity stories serve as litmus tests. On one side there are people who are genuinely interested in the fact that Paris Hilton was arrested. On the other side, there are people who are genuinely anxious to tell you about the absurdity of the story—and of the people who are interested in it. A big celebrity story allows those in the second group to remind themselves how smart they are and how they're so occupied thinking about things like NATO expansion that they don't have time to talk about such frivolity. Except, of course, for the hours they spend telling how silly the story is.

The media actually does this when it covers some of the stories. If you watched the coverage of Paris Hilton going to jail, you'd see almost every anchor all but apologizing for discussing the story. They rolled their eyes even as they covered the story wall-to-wall for a full day.

When I cover these stories I'm more interested in the fringe opportunists who swoop in to grab a piece of the action (much like yourself). What was the best part of O.J. being arrested in Las Vegas? Probably the guy from Jimmy Kimmel's show standing next to O.J.'s lawyer at a nationally televised press conference, cheering on the attorney and rightly making a mockery of the entire proceeding. (It also might have been the guys at the rehearsal dinner who O.J. talked into being his wingmen on the "sting operation").

It's the woman releasing the doves when Michael Jackson was acquitted. The stories themselves aren't interesting at all. What's at stake? Paris Hilton might go to jail for a couple of days? Who cares? Show me the sparsely-attended "Free Paris Now!" rallies. The main event is irrelevant. It's the sideshow (and freak shows) people are waiting to see.

I also asked him to comment on some of the dynamic fame trends we're seeing as a result of MySpace and YouTube. Here's his reply:

We had a woman named Tila Tequila on our show one night. She had become a huge celebrity with nothing more than a MySpace page. She had something like 250 million hits on her page. She was on magazine covers. She had endorsement deals. We wanted to get to the bottom of her fame. What did she do exactly? After a long interview, we still could not answer that question.

We learned a lesson that night—one that Paris Hilton had already begun to teach us. It doesn't matter why you're famous. It just matters that you are. If you have a computer, a gym membership, a clichéd tattoo on the small of your back, and a collection of bikinis, you too can become an international superstar. Now that I know who she is, I see Tila Tequila all over the place. I don't begrudge her that fame. She's only taking advantage of the times we live in. Good for her. It would be nice if she did something, though, you know? She should probably learn how to juggle or something.

129 ★

CHAPTER 7

Become Famous in Your Underwear
(Or, Getting Radio Coverage)

Anyone can be on the radio. Seriously. If you don't believe me, jump in your car and listen to your favorite local deejay interview someone you've never heard of before leading into the new Britney Spears single. These stations have a phenomenal amount of time to fill each day. Anything weird or out of the ordinary is a likely subject for a "local" show. And these shows are powerful in their markets: Even a brief deejay endorsement for your local business can be a life-altering event.

SECRET #36: HOW TO GET ON RADIO SHOWS

Guest spots on the morning drive-time shows are *not* simply reserved for A-list actors plugging their latest films! With the right pitch and a little enthusiasm, literally *anyone* can end up on these shows.

First, you need to understand the psychological state of most radio show hosts. Imagine if your daily routine consisted of reading traffic reports, regurgitating outdated weather forecasts, and actually using the words "hot" and "new" to introduce any song by Matchbox 20. You'd be understandably depressed and desperately on the lookout for *anything* exciting!

The mantra for getting radio coverage is: "Start local, go national." What this means is that you have a much better chance of landing a local show to begin with. Use these shows as practice. You'll learn to play with various on-air personas until you find one that feels right to you. Are you the cool, laid-back guest that listeners can relate to? Or, are you the aggressive and sarcastic guest listeners will remember for weeks to come?

Pitching a local show is not difficult. Find the station's website with a Google search. Go to the page of the deejay or host you think your pitch will resonate with the most. Often these pages include the email address of the host.

In your email, explain why what you have to say relates to the show's city. For example, let's say you're pitching a popular show in Washington, DC. If you grew up in DC and you are the author of a new book about your childhood, you would want to mention this. Tell a bit about how growing up in DC influenced you as a writer.

Find some way, *any* way, to make your pitch geographically relevant. If you're pitching a show in Atlanta, you need to figure out a way that having you on the show will interest listeners in the Atlanta area. Perhaps you bumped into a total stranger last time you were at Atlanta International Airport, and *now* the two of you are (somewhat) happily married. That delicious tidbit suddenly makes you relevant to the show's audience!

133 ★

The second part of your email should play up why you're an exciting guest to have on the air. Let your passion for your cause, business, or yourself come across naturally. Don't ramble, but give a few clear sentences showing off your energy. Nobody wants a boring guest on the air. People will switch over to another station or plug in their iPods, and radio hosts will never book a guest they think will lose their listeners.

Your "passion sentences" can be as simple as this: *I've been an ER doctor practicing in the Atlanta area for the past eight years, and let me tell you, the initial thrill of bringing a patient back to health still hasn't worn off!*

SECRET #37: MAKING THE MOVE TO NATIONAL SHOWS

When you have some local experience under your belt and are ready to pitch national shows, your appeal to the show should be similar—except instead of telling the host or producer why you'll interest listeners in a certain area, explain why you're a great fit for the show.

For example, if the host is known for a raunchy sense of humor and you're a sex therapist, mention this! Let them know that you've been a sex therapist for the past fifteen years *and* that you've accumulated the best sex joke collection ever.

Closing your email with "Here's my landline number" is a subtle way of showing that you're a pro: Radio shows hate to reach you on a cell phone because it sounds *awful* on the air. Even though you may think reception is fine on your phone, it sounds like you're being interviewed from the far side of the moon.

If you're called for a pre-interview, come across as enthusiastic and full of energy. You need to be at least minimally entertaining. Ask if the interview will be taped or live. If it's taped, they'll take the best parts of the interview and air that. If it's live, you need to be especially quick on your toes! Know your facts, have a sheet of paper in front of you with the key points you plan to get across in the interview, and let the host know *exactly* what you'd like them to plug. Helping other people succeed is one of the perks of being a popular radio host, so don't be shy about this.

It's cheesy—and sometimes pisses off producers—if you're answering questions with "Well, I say that in my book on page thirty-seven," or "Just go to the site for more information." You're on the air to provide information, not to redirect listeners to something. **Let the host do your plugging for you.**

A good host will plug your event, business, or book when they initially introduce you, and in subsequent introductions after commercial breaks. This is far more professional than you constantly mentioning your product, and it also lends more credibility: Many listeners are familiar with the host's voice and have been listening to him or her for *years,* so anything they plug is going to feel like a personal recommendation from a friend!

When it's time for your interview, just take a deep breath and remember that this should be fun above all else. Talk slowly and with a fair amount of confidence. It doesn't hurt to address the host by name once or twice during the interview—it shows listeners that you're "in the moment" and not just making the rounds of all the major shows as some actors do. I've heard interviews where an actor or musician was clearly just on a show because they had to be there, and it totally turned me off! The life of a successful publicity whore isn't all that hard, and it certainly shouldn't be considered a *chore* to plug your new movie to five hundred thousand listeners.

At some point, you may get called in for an in-studio interview as opposed to one over the phone—especially if you're in the same city as the station. The same rules apply: Have fun and talk slowly. Try to show up a few minutes early, and let the receptionist know you're there for an on-air interview. *Usually* you'll be on the guest sheet and things will go smoothly. Just to be safe, mention the show you're supposed to be on and at what time.

The secret for successful radio interviews is to realize you *deserve* to be on-air. If you've jumped through the initial hoops and are invited on as a guest, jettison any lingering self-doubt. You may not have a "name" for yourself just yet, but that one interview could be the chance to propel yourself to the next level. There is always room for fresh, new voices on the radio—think of how much time these shows have to fill up with talk *every single day.*

★ 136

HOWARD STERN—BUZZ MONGER, ALSO VERY RICH

Self-proclaimed "King of All Media" Howard Stern is an expert buzz builder. A mention on his show will sell twenty thousand copies of whatever you're hawking. That's without you even trying. What's his secret? To be honest, it's not the shock value. There are plenty of radio show hosts who traffic in the grotesque and the blatantly sexual, yet they don't draw even a fraction of Stern's listeners. Howard Stern will go down in the history textbooks as both America's highest-paid radio personality and as the single most-fined person in broadcast entertainment. He is without a doubt *the* reason Sirius Satellite Radio, his new home, received so much attention in the media.

So what's his secret? The answer is: Everything is about Howard Stern. The topics of discussion on his show are frequently about how something impacts *him*, whether it be disagreements with a network, or a tempting new offer, or an unpleasant run-in with someone in the public eye. This brand of egocentrism is actually magnetic. Over time, listeners develop a "relationship" with Stern, where they feel like they have a vested interest in his success—or, at the very least, a morbid curiosity to see what he does next.

137 ★

Now, don't get me wrong, I realize you can't be expected to create this sort of audience bond during a four- or five-minute radio interview. **Of course, you'll apply the basics: Speaking slowly and clearly, casually addressing the host by his or her first name, and being laid-back.** But this still won't give you the full opportunity to connect with people on a deeper level.

This is where online newsletters and blogging come into play. For the vast majority of us, we don't have our own radio show and *years* to build up listener loyalty. Not to mention a staff and a production budget.

SECRET #38: INTERNET MADE THE RADIO STAR—MERGING YOUR AUDIENCES FOR MAXIMUM EXPOSURE

The tool we have to build fan loyalty is the Internet. I mentioned earlier the power of free opt-in newsletter services like Google Groups and Topica. Now I want to talk about what I use, which is a professional-grade mail-merge system. And I want to show you how this can be used to maximize your radio appearances, believe it or not.

Mail-merge software inserts user information, such as a subscriber's first name, automatically into email I send out to all of my members at once. So thousands of people receive a message from me, telling them what I have in store for them, and it's addressed to their first names. This creates instant loyalty. Sure, people know it's just a technological trick, but they also know that I care—and that if they reply to my email, I'll actually read it.

Also, professional-grade newsletter management allows you to capture new users in all kinds of ways. When someone visits my blog, for example, they may see a "subscribe now" box where they enter their first name and email address. In addition, I run highly targeted ad campaigns, sometimes burning through thousands of dollars in a single week, where I'll promote a "landing page" with a description of my newsletter—and a convenient subscribe box on the page.

This way, I'm building a platform from the ground up. To make things even more extraordinary, I can queue up several messages at once and predetermine how much time should pass before each message gets sent out. This means my newsletter can continue to run smoothly even if I'm on vacation and don't have reliable access to the Internet.

You're probably wondering what all this has to do with radio interviews. I'll connect the dots in a second; just bear with me.

So you have this fantastic mail-merge and distribution system, and you're building loyalty with every message you send. As I previously suggested, write as if you're writing a personal letter to a friend. Don't write like a marketer— you're not there to hawk a book or a business. Your newsletter is designed primarily to build trust, to connect with people interested in your cause, and to *very* casually inform people about your products.

When I have something I want to promote in a newsletter, I'll often just close by saying, "Here's a link; check it out sometime if you want." It's laid back, I'm not twisting anybody's arm, and the rest of the email is jam-packed with useful tips on whatever the newsletter pertains to. So it creates real value for subscribers.

Now here's the radio trick: Mention your free newsletter during the on-air interview. Tell listeners *exactly* how to subscribe to your list, whether it be visiting a page on your site and entering an email address or simply sending a blank message to a certain address.

★ Plugging During a Radio Interview
Instead of plugging the holy hell out of your product, cause, or company (which is what every *other* guest ends up

139 ★

doing in some way or another), you know that you don't need the listeners to make a purchase today. You don't need them to see your movie today, to check out your book at Barnes & Noble, to visit your wine store. You just want them subscribing to your opt-in newsletter so they can receive more information from you. Just get them to your website—don't waste your time going on and on about what you want them to buy right this second. Once you've got an email address and a first name and they've opted in (given you explicit permission to email them), you have all the time in the world to convert them into fans, customers, or both.

SECRET #39: FAST, EASY, AND FREE—WORDS TO USE IN ALL YOUR ADS, BUT PARTICULARLY ON THE RADIO

★ | 140

Take a look at a print ad for something that involves a considerable amount of consumer risk. I like to look at credit-card ads, in part because I'm always looking for more credit to fuel my insane advertising expenditures, and in part because it's fascinating. A product that costs about two cents to make (a glossy plastic card with a magnetic strip on the back) is marketed as a powerful lifestyle *choice*. There are cards tied to dividend reward programs, frequent flier programs, alumni associations, the military, specific companies, and everything in between. Rapper Timbaland mentions a lack of an American Express card in a song about how he has no money. The card itself, featuring a proud Roman soldier, makes you feel like you're being inducted into some kind of ancient, moneyed aristocracy . . . But I digress.

All credit-card ads use the words fast, easy, and free. They also like to throw in the word "safe" for good measure. Recently, a credit-card company wanted me to tie my bank account to the card so I could set up automatic monthly payments. I read the promotional copy and I wasn't convinced. Then, in bold at the bottom, was this assurance: "It's easy and safe." *Ah, fine*, I thought to myself. *I'll do it.*

Those few words are often the difference between success and failure. Use them in your on-air interviews and in your newsletter copy. Talk about how something is fast, easy, or safe. Preferably all three: We are more rushed than ever these days, and we want solid assurances that whatever you're doing won't hurt us and won't take away much of our time. And of course, we want it to be easy.

★ The Difference between Radio and Print Power Words

I place a lot of text ads online, and because I'm often spending at least a few hundred dollars at a time, I can't afford for any one ad to fail. They all need to make back the original investment and then some. So I choose my ad text carefully. I do "micro-campaigns" of fifty or sixty dollars, where I test new ideas and see how they perform when shown to certain demographic and geographic target audiences.

Perhaps surprisingly, words like free, easy, and safe don't have much influence when it comes to getting clicks. It may calm people down and win them over, but "assurance" words don't encourage people to click on your ads. People naturally ignore ads and only click on something that seems irresistible. Therefore, I create irresistible ads.

My ads will frequently mention some sort of secret. Throw the word "secret" into *any* advertising campaign, and the clicks automatically go up! You know that heinously popular book *The Secret?* Some people would have you believe it's popular because of an Oprah plug and preposterously aggressive online viral marketing. That's wrong. It's popular because of the title alone. Who *doesn't* want to unravel a secret, let alone *the* secret? Plus the cover graphic is mysterious and vague—it could easily be mistaken for a *Da Vinci Code* movie poster.

Coming in a very close second, the word "trick" has a proven positive effect on my advertising campaigns. This is especially true when it's used in the context of tricking a particular group or "other." If you were to run the ad *"Trick Your Boss into Giving You a Raise"* on a career-related website, you would likely get phenomenal results. That's just an example, but it has all the elements of a red-hot advertising campaign. First of all, implied in the title is the *promise* that upon clicking that link, you'll learn how to *trick* your boss (whom most people wouldn't at all mind tricking!) into giving you a raise (there's a strong implied benefit for anyone who clicks the ad).

One more secret (ha!) would be this: You aren't learning or finding out anything new, you're *discovering* it. The word "discover" has a powerful effect on people. I think it's maybe because we feel that so much of our world is already discovered. The greatest "discovery" for most people is a dollar on the sidewalk or an unexpected text message from an ex-girlfriend. All lands have been conquered, science is at an awkward point where we understand so much and yet remain vulnerable to the common cold . . . and ubiquitous social networking sites make it nearly impossible to lead a private life. There's nothing to discover.

That's why people go a little crazy when they read the word "discover" in ad copy or when they hear you use that word on-air. Just the *possibility* of claiming something as your own is tempting. Think about it for a second. There's a major credit-card brand named Discover. There's the Discovery Channel. Every other medical ad wants you to "discover the benefits" of using their product.

143 ★

When you only have a *minute* or two on-air, you need to choose your words carefully. If using these words will help subconsciously influence someone into checking your company out further, it is definitely worth the effort.

New! That three-letter word, followed by the manic exclamation mark, is nothing new. Yet despite the fact that we've seen it *thousands* of times in advertising copy, it always catches us. We're deeply tempted by the idea of something new. If you're in the grocery store, you'll see all kinds of products claiming to be "*new!*" that aren't new at all. "*New, improved formula!*" is written on soap packages and toothpaste tubes, despite the fact that they seem exactly the same as they've always been. Still, it caught my eye, and it catches yours.

During your radio interview, you want to emphasize the newness of your cause. "We're a new war protest group with a lot of fresh ideas." "Our new fall lineup is making an impact already," etc.

People are actually sick of hearing about the same organizations, handful of predictable celebrities, and meticulously marketed politicians. They want to hear about new things and new ideas. So make this a major emphasis of any on-air interview. This addiction to newness is also exactly why YouTube and talent competitions (e.g., *American Idol*) will always be tremendously popular.

★ 144

CONSERVATIVE RADIO: THE RAVING LUNATIC PHENOMENON AND HOW TO GET ON BOARD

Don't.

SECRET #40: THE ADVANTAGES OF LATE-NIGHT RADIO

Drive-time radio is fast and glamorous. You get a phone call, you're notified that you're now on the air with so and so—you give a few interesting points, they laugh, you laugh, you answer a couple more questions. They say thanks, and you're done. You hang up, and your five minutes is over. You stop shaking. Then you rub your hands together, check your web stats later that day, and notice a 600 percent increase in traffic. Drive-time radio is all frenzy and excitement—and quick plugging. That's why you should make use of the "power words" I described above.

Now let's talk about late-night radio, shows like *Loveline* and *Coast to Coast AM with George Noory.* They give you an opportunity to really talk, and you have time to relax (but not too much!) and actually win over listeners. Boom, boom, *boom*—you list all your major points. You have a few commercial breaks in which you can collect your thoughts and ask the host what he really thinks. Late-night radio interviews are a lot of fun. They feel like real conversations, because that's exactly what they are. And if you get listeners hooked by the time your interview is finished, you've just won over a hundred thousand new people who will spread the word.

Unless you're a real pro or you already have a famous name, I feel like most drive-time guests say something to listeners—and it goes in one ear and out the other. Late-night radio is your chance to drive a point home. Repeat the same statistics or major points a few times. Some listeners may be joining the program midway through your interview, but also, in radio it's a well-known fact that listeners need to be told the same thing at least three times before they actually think about it. This is why you'll hear short ads during commercial breaks over and over again. Advertisers know that their message needs to be repeated because listeners won't "jump" the first time they're told to jump.

Late-night radio shows also give you time to build real rapport with the host of the show. If you're fascinating and bring something meaningful to the program—and if they like you on a personal level, that never hurts either—it's not uncommon for a host to extend an invitation to come back soon. And they mean this!

Each evening talk show has a distinct audience. *Coast to Coast AM*, for example, is in love with the bizarre. They'll discuss UFOs, interview New Age gurus, chatter about the paranormal. As with all your pitches, tailor these late-night radio pitches to the mood of the individual show. For *Coast to Coast AM*, for example, try to make it a little bizarre. Your pitch can't just be, "Hey, I like your show. Let's shoot the breeze for an hour on-air." You need to have some pressing or weird or entertaining anecdotes on tap. Mention a few of these in your initial pitch; save the rest for the actual interview.

SECRET #41: DEALING WITH HOSTILE HOSTS

Every once in a while, you may encounter a host who seems unusually hostile. The producer who invites you on is super nice, she's sure to mention that the host loves your book or your project, and then you get on and it's like, "What was I *thinking* to come on here?"

You're suddenly in a war zone. This happened to me once a couple years ago: It's probably the only interview friends of mine still talk about, because in retrospect, it was hilarious. When you're in the studio, though, it isn't hilarious. It's frightening. Someone is trying to ruin your image in front of thousands of people. This is where you stand your ground. You can even say, "I'm not sure why you invited me on if this is how you're going to be."

During a commercial break, tell the host to take it easy on you. If this doesn't work, just fight back. You can't curse, and you can't be *too* mean (listeners will think you're a jerk and won't sympathize with you), but you don't have to put up with a hostile host. If they talk over you, say, "I can't get a word in edgewise here, because you keep talking." At least that way listeners will know why you're not defending yourself.

Try to stay upbeat and humorous. And in the heat of battle remember that you're there to plug your cause! If the host is being a total jerk, then all etiquette rules go out the window. Don't listen or respond to them in any way—use your remaining minutes to plug whatever it is you're promoting in the first place.

Of course, this should not happen. Most hosts are professional and kind. But this advice is just in case you get a bad seed. Do your research; listen to past shows on the station's website, do a Google search on the host, ask the producer what the show's "tone" will be like. Ninety-nine-point-nine percent of the time you won't have to worry about this. But when it happens, do your best to put up a good fight. Don't lose your cool. And definitely plug your cause.

SECRET #42: WHY RADIO SELLS

We've already discussed this a bit, but it bears repeating:

Radio is a powerful medium for building buzz. It reaches a wide audience simultaneously, it has built-in credibility, and listener relationships with on-air personalities mean that they are likely to check you out further if the host plugs you well.

Radio is obviously an auditory medium: You only have to worry about speaking; it doesn't matter what you look like or how well you present. I've literally done successful radio interviews in my underwear before (it was a phone-in, not an in-studio!). If you can chat with someone on the phone, you can be successful at radio.

Also, radio gives you the opportunity to repeat yourself over and over again until you are actually heard. As I mentioned a bit earlier, **listeners need to hear something at least three times before they'll act on it.** Television, by contrast, is simply too fast-paced for you to effectively repeat yourself. Most guest segments are short, and the show has a definite direction: There's no way for you to link back to your major talking points.

Radio is also a lot of fun. TV may be glamorous, but radio feels extremely *natural*. You chat with someone, have a damn good time, and it just so happens that thousands of people are privy to your conversation at the same time (or later on, if it's taped). And since you can potentially do a lot of different radio shows in a short period of time, you have the luxury of testing out different approaches. Mention your cause directly in one interview, and in another interview, test out my idea of directing people to a newsletter sign-up web page. See which one has the biggest reaction.

SECRET #43: BRING YOUR "A-GAME" ON THE AIR

This is a quick tip sheet to look over immediately before you do an on-air interview. This way you'll have all your bases covered. Good luck!

1. **Be yourself.** Let your natural personality shine, and speak as you would to a friend. Unless you're on the BBC or NPR or something like that, radio is an informal and friendly medium. It's often colloquial. Remember not to curse; if swearing is a part of your personality, that's cool, but it's always best to keep it clean on-air.

2. **Address the host by name.** "Mike, you're absolutely right, that's exactly what we're trying to do," would be a good response. Avoid calling the host Mr. or Ms., and don't use "sir" or "ma'am" on the air—you may think you're being respectful, but it comes across as needlessly cheesy to listeners. It's stuffy: Radio is supposed to be fun and open.

3. **Know what you're going to say.** Once you're on the air, you should already know exactly what points you plan on getting across to listeners. Plan this out *beforehand:* Say your favorite phrase in front of a mirror a few times until you nail it. Prepare some index cards with a few points on each, and refer to them during your interview.

4. **Be upbeat!** Radio is, above all else, a lot of fun, and after you're through, you will have received more

149 ★

exposure than most businesses and individuals get in an *entire year.*

USE A LANDLINE, AND OTHER SEEMINGLY OBVIOUS TIPS

I've said this before, but don't forget it: **Use a land-line for radio interviews.** Don't think you can get away with using a cell phone. You'll sound like a war correspondent checking in from Iraq or something. You want your voice to be clear and crisp, which is why a regular phone is highly recommended for phone-in interviews.

Here's a bizarre secret: Take a hot shower before your interview. The heat and steam will relax you, plus it will clear up anything in your throat—your voice will sound better. Drink some water before an interview, especially if it's for a full-hour segment. I've found that a bit of green tea with honey also helps improve your voice.

Don't forget to tell everyone to listen in! If you have an opt-in newsletter, send out that blast telling everyone the station and air time. For those in other states and countries, send a link to the show's website. Many stations offer free online streaming so that you can listen in from anywhere.

If you're doing the interview from your home and you have a dog or other noisy pet, make sure it can't be heard on-air. Give it something to chew on or find an area of the house where you'll be relatively "sound-proofed." It's annoying and grotesquely unprofessional when you can hear a guest's dog barking in the background. Also, don't have the radio on in the background—there's no need to follow along; simply answer the host's questions.

CHAPTER 8

*Celebrity Tabloids: Getting in Them
or Staying out of Them*

It would be cool to be in a celeb tabloid, right? *In Touch, Life & Style, Us Weekly, People*—you know, the magazines that matter? We've all enjoyed these guilty pleasures at some point—the slightly worn copy in the doctor's office, the copy of *OK!* you surreptitiously bought in line at the supermarket last Wednesday, the impressively tall stack of *People* issues next to your toilet.

The point here is that even though these magazines are kinda trashy, and ultimately vacuous (how many times *can* you see the same celebrity walking along the beach with his kids?), they're also insanely popular, both in the United States and abroad. Europe, especially the UK, has its own crop of celebrities every bit as bizarre as ours. There's some crossover (Keira Knightley, Posh and Becks, the occasional band), but it's by no means 100 percent. Then there are the truly *international* tabloid staple brands like Paris Hilton, Angelina Jolie, and Brad Pitt. Everybody seems to care about these chosen few. But why? And can you benefit from celebrity tabloid coverage without their megawatt stardom?

SECRET #44: HOW TO GET IN THEM

Most of this book is pragmatic. If you follow the techniques outlined, you *will* get radio and television coverage—assuming you have a bit of luck and your pitch to producers is enticing enough. With the gossip glossies, your chances of getting in are slim to nil. Usually tabloid coverage is something that happens once you're already receiving attention from other outlets (radio, TV, gossip blogs). It doesn't happen on its own. This is because these magazines usually want to do stories on people everyone *already knows about*. This makes solid business sense: These magazines treat celebrities as "brands," and they want to feature brands that readers have actually heard of. Don't throw in the towel yet, however—there are still a few gambles that could pay off for you.

★ The first route: Date someone famous.

Since the tabloids are basically an ongoing national soap opera, your best bet is to "date into" the club. Bonus points if you cheat on them, fight frequently in public, or have a budding movie career.

★ The second route: Become a reality television star.

This is actually easier than it sounds: New reality shows are always looking for contestants. They get the semi-humiliating and hilarious footage (possibly at your expense) that they need for their show, it's relatively cheap for the network to produce, and *you* get instant stardom. Of course, most of these "stars" burn out and aren't able to make the leap to permanent fame, but while they're hot, the tabloids will cover them. Check MTV's casting call page at http://www.mtv.com/ontv/castingcall/ and the NYC television/film/radio casting call section on Craigslist at http://newyork.craigslist.org/tfr/frequently. With a little persistence, and a Faustian deal with a low-budget reality-TV production company, you could pull this one off.

★ **The third (and mostly secret) route: The Trojan Horse technique.**

When what you really want is exposure for your book or clothing line or music CD, why would you want to be featured in the tabloids—and thus have your private life exposed to public scrutiny? It would be far better to have a photo of an A-lister at the beach or by the pool enjoying your product. This is tricky and depends almost entirely on luck, but if you know anyone in the public eye, send them free copies of your wares. With a lot of luck, the paparazzi may snap a few photos of your celebrity friend enjoying your book/CD/clothing, etc.

SEXY SPICE, THE SKINNY BITCH

When international superstar Victoria Beckham was caught with the book *Skinny Bitch* in May 2007, the very next week it sold over forty thousand copies as a direct result! Having your product in a celebrity's sweaty hands is often enough to shove yourself into the mainstream. It's a strong endorsement, and yet it comes across as natural. The Trojan Horse technique can be invaluable, but it's also unpredictable. So send your book or product to more than one well-known person, because you never know who's going to connect with it—and carry it around.

These magazines also do book and DVD reviews—contact the editor in charge of these sections and get an address. Send him or her a free copy of whatever you're promoting along with a note explaining exactly why it is related to a celebrity the tabloid frequently covers. Since these publications have huge readerships, a single positive blurb in one will be enough to put you on the map. Plus it increases the likelihood of celebrities checking out your book or product and eventually endorsing it, either directly or just by being photographed near it.

SECRET #45: NOW, WHY TABLOIDS DON'T MATTER UNLESS YOU'RE BRAD PITT OR ANNA NICOLE'S BABY

Ultimately, the tabloids aren't your best marketing vehicle. In the vast majority of cases, as I've said, you need to be already well-known before the tabloids will cover you. They're extremely hard to get into and risky, and sometimes the coverage doesn't stop even when you want it to (you've seen it—they'll publish unflattering photos of you, follow you around during a personal crisis—tabloid coverage can become a never-ending nightmare).

Your energy is far better spent trying to land radio and television appearances—and building up your online presence *every single day*. If my newsletter has less than three hundred new sign-ups on a weekday, a little part of me dies inside. OK, that's sarcastic, but I truly do place an emphasis on growing my newsletters. Your online presence is a sure bet that will keep the buzz going and will lead to bigger and better things. Better yet, you can both initiate and control (to a certain extent) your online ventures. And once you've built a significant online following, whenever you have a new viral video or product to promote, you already have a huge, captive audience of loyal fans who will quickly spread the word for you.

Tabloids are very much an "old Hollywood" idea: You're either in or you're out. The editors are writing stories about you or they aren't. With online buzz methods, nobody else decides. You do. It all comes down to how savvy and persistent you're willing to be. I prefer these odds to the whims of a callous tabloid editor.

PARIS HILTON—BUZZ WHORE, ALSO GENIUS

Paris Hilton embodies tabloid culture. She's eminently photogenic, she has global brand name recognition, and there's always some kind of controversy to write about—her stint in jail, her mysterious falling-outs with LA "frenemies," the embarrassing website that revealed the contents of her storage closet. **But let's not forget what made Paris Hilton a tabloid icon in the first place.** Her ubiquitous sex tape vaulted her to international celebrity—she already had the name, the looks, and the money, and then the sex tape created the perfect scandal for the tabloids. Sex appeal, conflict, and mystery all rolled into one convenient package. And the tape was intrinsically viral in nature—all over the Internet within a few hours of its discovery.

I hate to say it, because this is an extremely sleazy way to go about getting attention for yourself, but if you're on the fringe of making the A list (or the B list), a DUI or sex tape will boost your recognition like nothing else. The tabloids aren't classy. They want grit and embarrassment, preferably at your expense. This is a path to fame that some would say Paris Hilton has pioneered.

SECRET #46: FLYOVER STATES—WINNING HEARTS AND MINDS WITH TABLOID PHOTOS

When I lived in Missouri, the tabloids kept me sane. I felt starved for useless celebrity details any time I was away from New York for a few months. Luckily, *In Touch* was there (only $1.99!) to keep me, well, you know, in touch with everything. Every Wednesday or Thursday I'd hit the local grocery store and pick up the new issue. And not only are tabloids addictive, but they keep you up to speed for water-cooler conversations. If someone mentions how Orlando Bloom was good in that one movie, you can bust out your knowledge about whomever he's dating and what he did at the club last week.

Talking about politics often leaves people feeling deflated and somewhat depressed, but gossiping about celebrities puts everyone in a better mood! Tabloids are a continuation of the gossip you experience firsthand in high school. In adult life there isn't as much to gossip about—people paying their mortgages, going to the Bahamas once a year, that's about it. The tabloid industry gives you something intriguing and new to chatter about each week, with the added benefit that everyone else knows exactly who you're talking about.

SECRET #47: SMILING AND THE PDA POSE

Everybody in the tabloids is smiling, all the time. This makes life seem cheerful and bearable. Even when the article is about a divorce or something equally depressing, the accompanying photo will be of the celebrity in question smiling, waiting in line for a cup of Starbucks. So if you ever find yourself posing for the tabloids, make a point of smiling. It will get people to root for you. Over time, readers identify with celebrities who match their values. This is why women will sometimes say things like, "My friends tell me I look like Angelina Jolie," even though nothing could be further from the truth! And why guys will make claims like, "I've been told I'm a lot like Clive Owen." (Umm, no!) People have surprisingly strong bonds to the people they read about. Their lives are glamorous, conflict-ridden, and polarizing all at the same time. You may like Ryan Phillippe's movies and therefore be a fan, while a good friend of yours could hate him and say, "I can't believe he did that to Reese Witherspoon! What a dirtbag." See how oddly polarizing the tabloids can be—and how passionate people can feel about them, even though they've never met the people they're talking about?

Anyway, this chapter is obviously a flight of fancy—your chances really aren't good—but should you ever find yourself frequently in the tabloids, **always carry a PDA with you.** You need to have a BlackBerry or iPhone on you at all times! This way, if you're caught doing something lame (in line at the DMV, for example), you can whip out your BlackBerry Curve and at least *pretend* to be closing some important business. Always appear busy. Tabloids celebrate a high-stakes, fast-paced lifestyle—if you want to stay in them, you need to live up to this expectation.

161 ★

CHAPTER 9

Building the Empire, Maintaining Coverage, and Avoiding Burnout

So you've made it. Congratulations! People know who you are, or at least they're beginning to, and you have enough connections to get coverage when you have something to promote. Let's talk about how to maintain. In all things, you either grow or you shrivel up and die. I read that in a cheesy self-help book, but it's definitely true when it comes to buzz. Unless you're expanding, you're fading. A runaway YouTube hit—hell, even a successful TV series—can only take you so far. You need to build the empire. You need to work on your "brand image" and find new markets, just as any good brand would do.

SECRET #48: WHY OVEREXPOSURE SUCKS—AND AVOIDING IT

★ Nobody Likes an Overbearing Buzz Whore

There's a difference between expanding your fan base and over-connecting with the people you've *already* got on your side. In other words, don't preach to the choir. When someone signs up for my newsletter, for example, the system sends them one message per day from me—but only for the first seven days. This way, they get a feel for the newsletter's content and my style, but then it tapers off sharply. The mailings go down to one new message per every couple weeks at the most. This way, subscribers genuinely look forward to hearing from me—I'm a welcome ten-minute break from the mundane obligations of school or work. I'm not a constant presence. In other words, I'm not an overbearing or "over-eager" presence. If it comes between giving someone a little too much of you or not quite enough, go for the latter. Most of the time, however, the problem is not that you're too eager. It's that you're being overexposed—you've attained some degree of notoriety, and now the media is simply talking about you too often. This can have negative effects.

★ Dodging Constant Exposure

Some psychologists say that familiarity is actually a good thing (as opposed to breeding contempt), and while that's true—people need to know who you are to invest in your brand—too much familiarity is a bad thing. I think we all have one or two people we hate simply by virtue of constantly seeing them on television. This is part of the reason why television show hosts are, for the most part, meticulous in their presentation. There's something invasive about someone talking at you every morning, even if it's just TV. These are your only free minutes before work, a short period of time when you can sip your coffee, sift through your unpaid bills, and think about what you want to do with your day. Any show that invades your sacred downtime better be good. So you have to master being familiar without being too familiar.

Email marketing, if that's what you want to call it, is very similar. You want the "new message" icon to get people excited when they open a new email message from you. You want readers to be excited when they see that you're quoted in a story or that your business is mentioned as a hot spot. But your coverage should be occasional and unexpected.

Everybody wants to punch a winner. That's basically what director/producer Judd Apatow said in a recent magazine interview: He had two successful films come out in one summer (*Knocked Up* followed by the hilarious *Superbad,* which he produced), and he was distinctly aware of the fact that people will grow sick of you if all they hear is success, success, success. Have a few failures, hopefully manageable ones, or just drop below the radar for a while. All I mean by this, in most cases, is show a little human weakness. People love to hear stories of how your movie almost didn't get the funding it needed, how the first few months of business were rough on you, etc. If you aren't willing to show any weakness whatsoever, then at least act grateful. But remember that people like to root for an underdog.

THE SELF-DEPRECATING GENIUS OF SETH ROGEN AND JUDD APATOW

While we're on the topic of *Superbad,* the cast of that movie had a convincing back story. Seth Rogen co-wrote the script with childhood friend Evan Goldberg when they were both angsty teens growing up in Vancouver—as Rogen has said in interviews, he started the script when he was twelve years old. And his life was every bit as awkward as the experiences in *Superbad*—this kind of admission creates a connection with fans. It's hard to hate someone who profits from his own past weaknesses!

Judd Apatow also hilariously mentioned in a June *Rolling Stone* interview that he got into comedy writing as a result of being humiliated so many times in school, always getting picked last for school teams, etc. He told the interviewer that he was literally picked after girls and "people with broken arms." Funny to hear that kind of self-deprecation from an immensely successful Hollywood producer. If you're going to be constantly in the public eye for a while, at least be fun—give people a reason to root for you.

SECRET #49: EASY WAYS TO PROFIT FROM RECOGNITION—THE REAL WORLD HAS-BEEN CAST MEMBER PHENOMENON

Even reality television stars, the lowest rung on the fame ladder, can get "appearance fees" for showing up at launch parties and corporate events. Basically, you can be paid to get drunk and take a few photos. Not a bad life for a has-been!

167 ★

There's a critical point where your online success can be transformed into real-world notoriety. It is impossible to put an exact number on this, because it really depends. Once your blog is getting fifty thousand or a hundred thousand loyal readers per day, does this help you break out into offline media? Of course it does. *Who* reads your blog matters almost as much as how many people are reading it. For example, the TV news industry blog TVNewser.com ostensibly has some influence among television producers (since they read it), even though it isn't a particularly high-traffic blog overall. Galleycat.com, a blog covering the publishing industry, is read by agents and editors in New York—thus a feature there can potentially help build your book's buzz even though it doesn't boast as many readers as, say, Daily Kos or Huffington Post.

Build up your online presence to the point where your platform will lead to a book deal. If you're an Internet celebrity, you're virtually guaranteed a decent deal—Tucker Max, Maddox, that dude who had people send him postcard confessions (it turned into the massively popular *PostSecret* series of books—see how *secret* is in the title?), and just about every blogger with a readership more than five thousand people. A book deal gives you legitimacy and a way to extend your brand offline. People in bookstores will find out about you, even if they've never read your blog or newsletter before.

★ 168 **Consulting is another way to make some serious bank.** If you've starred in a YouTube short that got a few million views, this makes you valuable to viral marketers. Just about every large company is trying to jump on the viral bandwagon, and it won't be hard to find someone willing to finance your next video idea.

So there's the leap from blogging to print. There's also the massive leap from video blogging (vlogging, as the kids call it) to mainstream on-air talent. Amanda Congdon, former host of the online-only *Rocketboom*, a low-budget newscast, eventually snagged top-notch representation by Endeavor (a top Hollywood talent agency) and is now ABC News's video blogger.

DANE COOK AND RADIOHEAD: THE INTERNET FARMING SYSTEM

In this new world of dynamic fame, numbers are everything. If you can prove that your viral videos or blog posts are reaching a substantial audience, this will lead to bigger and better things. It's a sort of "farming system" where the best of the online world eventually break into the mainstream. Dane Cook established himself this way. He invested some of his own money in building up a Web presence, he posted his funniest material on MySpace, and now he's a major force in comedy—an HBO special, star of several major motion pictures, not to mention his wildly popular CD *Retaliation.* In a lot of ways, Cook is the perfect example of dynamic fame. And he understands exactly how to take online success and build it into a true empire. There isn't a college student in America who hasn't heard his CD at least once.

169 ★

More peculiar is the trend of mainstream talent going online to build a stronger niche audience. Mega-popular group Radiohead released their newest album exclusively online, allowing fans to "decide" how much they were willing to pay for the download (those strapped for cash could download it for free). In exchange, downloaders gave Radiohead an email address, a postal address, and some other basic info—no doubt a great way for the band to keep in touch with fans and promote future tours! At the same time, direct online distribution of the album cut out any middlemen—iTunes, the record companies, retail stores like Best Buy, etc. This means higher profit margins for the band.

SECRET #50: FINDING YOUR NICHE

When you build your online newsletter and manage your online buzz campaigns, don't go off in ten different directions. Focus on an area that fascinates you, and become an expert in that area. You'll build a fiercely loyal audience within your niche, and then later on, you can enlist their help. They can help you make the leap to the mainstream—but first you need to carve out your own piece. Even Donald Trump didn't start as a global brand: He focused on something he knew well, real estate, and made his name that way. Howard Stern didn't start off as the "King of All Media"—he grew into that role after years of focusing on his best strength: Outrageous, self-involved talk radio.

Especially with the free buzz tools available to us online, it's tempting to go off in too many different directions. Resist that urge. Focus on a key area, and exploit the living hell out of it. I belong to a high-end gym back at home in Annapolis, and the owner there realizes her strength is in "health-conscious" offerings—yoga, acupuncture, healthy living seminars, massage therapy, Pilates. I admit it's not exactly the most masculine gym, but she isn't trying to win everyone over: She goes for a very specific type of person and then uses a targeted newsletter system to keep them informed of new classes that open up at her center, free events that she hosts, and so forth. It keeps the gym's members involved. If she were to rapidly expand the gym in all directions, trying to capture market share from the larger "meathead" gyms in the area, she would alienate all of the wheatgrass-shot drinking, dabbling in Kabbalah, yoga-mat owning members. She knows her strength, and she sticks to it.

DONALD TRUMP—BUZZ WHORE, ALSO SPECTACULAR BRAND

I keep saying there's going to be a Donald Trump backlash at some point, but it never comes. People can't get enough of his hard-hitting commentary, no-nonsense attitude, and blatant self-promotional swagger. The market for Donald Trump's semi-motivational books, such as the humbly titled *Think BIG and Kick Ass in Business and Life*, seems to be limitless.

Donald Trump is a human brand that fires on all cylinders—marketing, buzz whoring, merchandising, platform development—so it's no wonder that he is mentioned throughout this book. It's something of a paradox, if you think about it: Do people buy his stuff because he's successful, or is he successful because people keep buying his properties and books? It's like asking which came first, the chicken or the egg. Trump is no longer chiefly a real-estate mogul or even a businessman: I would argue he's a buzz genius, more interested in taking up real estate in your mind than in your city. He understands that if you know him, if you connect with what he represents on some level, you'll buy his condos and drink his vodka and watch his television shows. Making the sale is secondary; making the connection is primary.

MARTHA STEWART—SAME DEAL, EXCEPT WITH A VAGINA

If Donald Trump has the market cornered on guys who brag about where they went to business school and refer to women exclusively as "chicks," Martha Stewart enjoys market dominance among women who read catalogs, care about cooking, and participate in anything even remotely domestic. Martha Stewart's TV show is simply called *Martha*—as if you're going over to your friend Martha's house on a warm afternoon, hoping to get some advice on whether you should keep the curtains or not. That smile greets you as she gets to work on her latest on-air concoction. Martha Stewart doesn't have doubts, at least not on her show: What she does is simply *the way* it's done.

Thanks to her imprisonment, and the widespread media attention she received because of it, even guys like me—of the Trump persuasion—are aware of her. She's extended her brand far beyond the set of busy women who watch her show and devour her magazine articles. If I'm at a store and I see a Martha-branded item for my apartment, I'm likely to pick it over almost any other brand. She owns real estate in my mind, just like Trump does.

> New York City artist Delavega occasionally hangs a sign outside of his store that simply says, "I just bought real estate in your mind." It's simple, but profound—passersby have their thoughts momentarily "hijacked" by the sign, and they are now aware of an artist that fifteen seconds before they may not have known about. Awareness is a key part of any successful human brand.

Martha Stewart is also a good example of niche buzz. The jail fiasco was manna from the buzz gods, but even without that chapter in her life, she would have remained a highly marketable celebrity. Rather than some public personalities who are known for everything (and therefore nothing), Martha Stewart occupies a niche. She has a built-in audience of people passionately interested in what she does.

173 ★

SECRET #51: PROPER PRODUCT ENDORSEMENT

Once you've hit it pretty big, people will likely start approaching you and asking you to endorse their products with your name and image. When you pick products to endorse, they should enrich your personal brand—think Tiger Woods with Nike. If you aren't discriminating, you'll become known as a "sell-out" who will endorse anything.

This means you'll have to turn down offers once you're famous, which means losing out on money in the short term. But it's important to make conscious decisions and treat your name with respect. If you dilute your brand to the point where you're a self-promotional joke, you won't be able to land lucrative endorsement deals in the future. Don't sell yourself short—only identify with companies and products that resonate with you as a person. You don't want to be like the washed-up athletes you see on local TV commercials for car dealerships!

GEORGE FOREMAN AND HIS GRILLS

There's product endorsement out there that doesn't really make sense. Paris Hilton's infamous Carl's Jr. commercial, for instance, doesn't really make sense. It got a lot of people talking—which is good—but there was no real fit. Do you honestly think a skinny heiress slams big, greasy cheeseburgers from Carl's Jr.?

However, there are some personal brand extensions that make perfect sense. The George Foreman Grill may be the best example. First of all, it's well designed. There's a grease pan, it takes only a minute to set up, and the steaks don't taste half-bad. It's easy to use—just plug it into a wall socket. And it's a perfect match for George Foreman. The Grill is uber-masculine—it's not called the Sarah Jessica Parker Grill for good reason.

SECRET #52: MERCHANDISING, MERCHANDISING, MERCHANDISING

When you reach a certain level of fame, people may seek out products simply because they are associated with you. While things like a hat with your name on it *may* attract some buyers and put some money in your pocket, there's another route.

One thing you may not have thought about: You can provide "digital merchandise" to your fans. While physical merchandise has some drawbacks (you need to pay someone to create branded hats, T-shirts, whatever else—and there's no guarantee they will sell), digital merchandise has none. A digital product, such as a webcast, e-book, or paid access to certain areas of your website, costs you very little. And demand will increase as your fame does.

175 | ★

VISITING BILLOREILLY.COM AND GETTING FACTOR GEAR

Bill O'Reilly's website is a good example of online brand extension—and digital merchandising. People who actually enjoy his show (they're out there some-where) visit his website and sign up for a "premium" paid membership. This gives them a more direct way to contact Bill, should they feel the urge to do so, and they also receive access to his op-ed articles before the general public.

This is a super-smart way to profit from your most loyal fans—and to make them even more loyal. Of course, you could argue that keeping access free is sometimes better. Thousands of people read Zach Braff's blog to stay up to date on his new projects, but how many of those people would actually pay to read it? It is sometimes better to keep things *free* so you can reach the widest number of potential supporters. When you put a price on content, you're losing the 90 percent of people who simply won't pay. This is stupid: These are people who aren't willing to pay *right now*. That doesn't mean they won't pay for your products at some point in the near future—once they are more familiar with you. This is why my newsletters are always free. I don't care about making the sale. I only care about building familiarity and relationships with readers. Who knows what I'll be promoting tomorrow anyway? It's far better to have lifetime supporters rather than one-time sales.

Bill O'Reilly also sells "Factor Gear" on his website—all kinds of branded merchandise. Everyone loves buying something *physical*—hence the success of eBay. You open your wallet, and you're paying for the satisfaction of getting something in a little brown UPS box three days later. Physical items are always fine to sell, so long as access to you remains free on things like your website and in your newsletter. For example, you presumably paid for this book. It's a physical product, so the transaction made sense to you. I haven't in any way limited my fan base by selling this book. If you weren't yet "convinced," you could subscribe to my newsletter for free. You could email me for free or visit my websites. Access to content should remain free (unless you're extremely well known), especially when you're trying to build your personal brand into a globally known entity.

But don't take my word for it. Look at the Internet's greatest companies. Google offers gigabytes of email storage space for free. Yahoo! does the same thing. *The New York Times* website recently stopped its dumb practice, called Times Select, of charging for certain articles. Now the entire website is free.

To summarize here: Feel free to sell products, but never charge for mere access to you unless you get to Bill O'Reilly's point. If you already have two million viewers a night, you can provide additional content for a fee; otherwise, focus on expanding and keeping access to you free. Keep a line of communication open between you and your fans. It's pretty exciting if you're at the point where your biggest concern is how to profit from your celebrity.

CHAPTER 10

Other Sparkling Pearls of Wisdom

In the course of writing this book, and during my own journey as a buzz whore, I've developed some ideas that don't really fit into the earlier chapters. But they still may help you come up with a killer hook. So I've included them below.

SECRET #53: STAGE AN EVENT

Members of the media are constantly inundated with faxes, email, and phone calls announcing new products. To make your release stand out, try staging an event with a specific time and place. This gives local newspapers and area TV stations something to actually cover.

For example, if you're opening a wine store, a release simply announcing that you now exist is not likely to get significant coverage. Instead, organize a South American vineyard-tasting event at your store to kick things off. Let any blogs focused on your state know about the event at least two days in advance. Call and email all of the local papers with details—and it's okay to hit more than one contact within a news organization. For instance, if you send it to both the features writer and the local events reporter, you have a better chance of making it into the paper. At the very least, most community newspapers will include you in their events section. Many will opt to send out a features reporter and photographer, in which case have a few convincing quotes on tap!

In terms of taking the wine store coverage national, you need to ask yourself two questions: First of all, do I *need* national coverage? If you're simply a neighborhood wine shop, you'd be better served by focusing on local publicity. At the end of the day, your motivation should be making the store profitable, not necessarily becoming a celebrity—only go national if that's what your company needs in order to succeed.

Secondly, if you *do* want the national coverage (maybe your wine shop accepts orders via a website or toll-free number), find a way that you can be of use to reporters at the national level. Every couple years a story comes out announcing some new health benefit of drinking red wine . . . the next time one of these stories hits the wire, build on it (Rule #2). Be aggressive and let the national networks know about your store. Play up your experience with red wine and say that you'd be willing to let camera crews come to your store. TV shows are always looking for the visual element: This helps them create a nice clip to go along with an otherwise bland story about wine antioxidants!

The secret here is to *think* like a successful television producer, not like a common self-promoter. The show's producers don't really care about sending business your way; they just want a captivating package to air. If you can help them add value to their piece, you stand a good chance—and you'll reap the rewards of exposure.

A HARLEY-DAVIDSON EVENT

I recently came across a fascinating article on MSN Money that shows exactly how staging an event can benefit you or your company.

> Harley-Davidson, the legendary American motor-cycle company, has begun staging "garage parties" exclusively for women. The idea here is that female bike enthusiasts can come together and talk shop—asking and answering technical motorcycle questions without being ridiculed by "know-it-all" tough guys.
>
> This "women-only garage party organized by the maker of heavyweight bikes" seems kind of unusual at first, but as you read the article, you realize that it's a brilliant idea. It draws in a potentially huge segment of new motorcycle owners, it costs almost nothing for Harley-Davidson to set up, and it results in serious press (MSN is a major Internet portal).
>
> Read the whole article here:
>
> http://articles.moneycentral.msn.com/Investing/Extra/HarleyToWomenHearUsRoar.aspx?page=1

★ 182

SECRET #54: THE ULTIMATE EVENT: "VS."

As consumers of news media, we love to hear about feuds and rivalries! It's human nature, after all, to watch to find out what happens in these situations—and talk about the fight with your friends. Also, finding an "other" to fight against will help keep you motivated. It will take your pitch from yet-another-publicity-grab to the realm of high drama. So find a way to be outraged!

Which of the following pitches is more likely to resonate with TV stations in your area? "Local Bakery Profits

Lowest In Past Five Years" or "Local Bakery Owner Vows to Run Rival Chain Panera Out of Town"—one is bland, the other is incendiary. Viewers are instantly asking themselves: What's wrong with Panera? What makes this other bakery better? Do I know anyone who has been there? I should check it out!

The importance of controversy in your pitch cannot be overemphasized. The news covers conflict: Wars, corporate fraud, disease, celebrity feuds, forest fires. The news is a product that people *choose* to tune into; if it were not filled with conflict, people would change the channel to their favorite drama on TV. Or they'd read the new thriller by Stephen King on the subway, as opposed to the morning paper.

183 ★

SOME RECENT CELEBRITY FEUDS

Donald Trump vs. Rosie O'Donnell. This particular bloodbath started when Rosie criticized Donald on *The View*—she basically said he was not one to pass moral judgments on others, which was a response to his somewhat sickening "pardon" of Miss USA Tara Conner. The rest is television history. The two went back and forth with a series of increasingly vulgar personal attacks, keeping them in the public eye for far longer than most of us cared to see!

Tom Cruise vs. Brooke Shields. This controversy started when Cruise condemned Shields for her publicly shared belief that antidepressants can be effective—I'm sure you remember the publicity war that ensued. While this did *nothing* to help Cruise's image, it put antidepressant use in the public eye, and it probably didn't hurt sales of Brooke's book about postpartum depression.

Donald Trump vs. The World. If you're looking for ways to create media controversy, look no further than Trump. Aside from trashing Rosie O'Donnell, Trump won't hesitate to speak bluntly about almost any celebrity. More often than not, he says the things you wish you could say yourself! When asked about *The View*'s Elisabeth Hasselbeck, he didn't hesitate to crown her as "one of the dumber people on television."

The secret here is obvious: Have an enemy. If you have no enemies whatsoever, create one. Usually this is not necessary, because with any amount of digging, you'll find a genuine enemy. We live in a competitive society, and there is *someone* out there who wants your business, your fame, or your expertise. Rivalries are pure publicity gold.

SECRET #55: SINCERITY—I REALLY MEAN IT

In October 2007, wildfires ravaged California. FEMA, the same federal agency that botched the Katrina relief effort, was charged with handling the fires. On October 23, they gave a press conference that the media soon reported was "fake"—there were no actual journalists in the room, just a bunch of FEMA staffers lobbing softball questions to their boss.

This story, because it is inherently ridiculous, received *far* more mainstream media attention than it would have if FEMA had just held a regular press conference in the first place. It became an instant scandal, making the agency seem hilariously inept at doing its own job.

Keep things honest; That's my last pearl of wisdom for you. You know how the *Anderson Cooper 360* tag line is "Keeping them honest"? Well, keep yourself honest. It's totally cool to spin something in a better or more interesting light—that's a fundamental part of buzz marketing. After all, what's so exciting about a ninety-second YouTube clip or a carbonated energy drink or the fact that one day a certain celebrity forgot to wear her underwear? It's the spin, the commentary, and the hype that interests us. As a prominent television producer explained in an earlier chapter, the stories themselves *aren't* all that interesting. It's the people on the sidelines who *contribute* to the story by doing something a little peculiar that interest people—the "fringe opportunists," as he calls them. Fringe opportunists eventually become simply opportunists, and then eventually they morph into stories themselves. They become the center of attention.

However, while you're styling yourself as a fringe opportunist, you still have to keep things honest. Blatant falsehood (like the author who had people convinced Katie Holmes hated her book) rarely works out in your favor. Some spin is encouraged and necessary, but spin is a far cry from outright lying. Have you looked at the lineup of guests on *The O'Reilly Factor* lately? It's supposed to be the "no-spin zone," yet most of the guests are master spin artists. They're buzz whores of the highest order!

NYGirlofMyDreams

A good, recent example of the sincerity rule is the story of Patrick Moberg. After sitting across from a girl with a flower in her hair on the subway, whom he allegedly fell in love with at first sight, he created a web page called NYGirlofMyDreams.com. On the page he posted a childish but endearing sketch of her and implored readers to help him find her. The site was featured on many popular blogs, including Gawker, and in a picture-perfect ending, his "dream girl" eventually received word of the page through a friend and emailed Patrick. The two went out for coffee and supposedly hit it off. They appeared on *Good Morning America* to share their sincere yet kinda awkward story of love at first sight.

SECRET #56: Learn from YouTube

Required Viewing

Pay close attention to this section. These are fun YouTube videos, and they're important viewing in the sense that they'll give you a good feel for what makes something viral.

So set aside an hour when you won't be disturbed, and check out these videos.

Keepon Dancin's Spoon Music Video

Do a search on YouTube for "spoon keepon dancin don't you evah" and you'll find this one. It's an immensely popular music video produced with the help of *Wired* magazine. In the video, a yellow sponge robot dances to a song by the group Spoon. The robot has motion sensors and can also detect sounds—it seems eerily aware of its surroundings when it dances. I'm not making this up! The video is oddly entertaining and has enjoyed immense viral popularity as a result.

Don't Tase Me, Bro!

Okay, you already know what this one is about. Watch the original on YouTube (search for "don't tase me"), and also check out the numerous remixes—for some reason, this thing took off like crazy!

Artist on Artist: Wes Anderson and Owen Wilson

You actually have to search for this one on MySpaceTV.com, as it's an exclusive on their site. It's a peculiar interview between director Wes Anderson and the hilarious Owen Wilson, a popular plug for the movie *Darjeeling Limited.* Among the best parts: A section in the middle when Owen Wilson talks about how the monkeys he encountered while shooting in India didn't have his "best interests at heart" and the assertion that monkeys "want to replace you." It's absurd and great!

The Landlord

You need to find this one on FunnyOrDie.com, although you can probably find it on YouTube as well. It's a short comedy skit starring Will Ferrell. It was supposedly conceived and shot in around forty minutes: It received millions of hits. Just goes to show you that sometimes the best viral ideas don't take very long to execute; it's about the immediacy of the idea and the interest that it generates, not necessarily the quality of the finished product.

Salad Fingers

A profoundly creepy series of short animated videos starring a character named "Salad Fingers." Hundreds of thousands of people are familiar with Salad Fingers; the cartoon is *so* bizarre that viewers feel compelled to share the link with others. Do a search on YouTube for "salad fingers" and all of the episodes will pop up. Watch as many as you can stomach.

CHAPTER 11

Peacing Out, Closing Thoughts,
and Publicity Zen

Now you know everything I do. Well, 99 percent, anyway. Here are my closing thoughts on buzz and a bit of publicity Zen. Creating buzz and media-whoring may be a lot of fun and can be quite profitable, but it can also be stressful. Producers will test the limits of your sanity, interviews will get mercilessly rescheduled, newspapers will blatantly misquote you, bloggers will disparage you. Welcome to the club of those who are in the public eye.

SECRET #57: PUBLICITY—IT'S A TWENTY-FIRST CENTURY ART FORM

In ancient times, there was no such thing as mass media. You either found out about someone through word of mouth, you met them in person, or you attended an event sponsored by them (think of the Coliseum in Rome and how emperors provided "bread and circuses" for the citizenry). Even if you were a peasant or a slave, there was often less separation between you and those who were talked about. You would see them passing by in a heavily guarded convoy, you would hear them give a speech, or a friend would tell you about their real, live experience with a certain "celebrity."

Skip ahead to the signing of the U.S. Constitution. The Federalist Papers were widely disseminated and served as a great buzz-marketing tool to increase support for a strong federal system. That was a great way to promote your cause back then, but had they been published in the twenty-first century, James Madison and Alexander Hamilton *certainly* would have run an accompanying blog with user comments enabled!

Look at how far we've come in the effectiveness of our promotional machines. We spend our time talking about people—politicians, world leaders, Hollywood brand names—yet most of us haven't met any of them. Despite this, we know ridiculous amounts about them. The tabloids publish pictures of embarrassing moments on the beach; the blogs quote things better left alone (for some!); television programs tell us where someone stands on major issues. And if the celebrities we're reading about, listening to, or watching are the kind of people we *like* at a gut level, they become the actor whose movie we'd run out to see on opening day or the charismatic politician who renews our excitement in the political game. It's not so much about people's talents these days—it's about who they are and how their audience feels about them.

Admit it: You have an opinion on Barack Obama, Larry King, Paris Hilton, and Britney Spears. You probably know more about Lindsay Lohan's personal life than you do about some members of your own family! I'm not saying you have too much time on your hands; I'm saying this is just the way it is. Celebrity culture is an inextricable part of modern life, and publicity is a uniquely American art form in a lot of ways.

Certain members of the media are revered, while others are despised. It's amazing how much we care about mainstream media—and how the line between celebrity and those covering it becomes blurred. It's also amazing how easy it is to become a part of this fascinating, ongoing dialogue. Even if you just have a blog or a column in your local newspaper, you're now a part of the media, a member of a great machine that is at times propaganda, at times public service, and at times pure entertainment.

I love to go to baseball games, but not for the reasons most people enjoy watching the game. I'm fascinated by the sheer amount of advertising we're exposed to at a baseball game. Advertising, much like publicity, has become such a crucial part of our daily lives that it too is an art form. Huge corporations and multinational banks are paying big bucks to take over a few neurons in my mind while I'm just trying to follow the game. It's an expensive, glamorous, never-ending battle for attention.

I like Times Square in New York for the same reason. Nothing charges up my batteries more than an afternoon visit there—the scrolling tickers, the national TV studios, the unimaginably expensive and well-designed electronic billboards everywhere. A battle is being waged for our attention. We're fiercely fought over every minute of the day, and we don't even realize it.

The cool thing is that my promotional techniques can allow you to compete with the massive, faceless companies who buy billboard advertising. They pay millions; you pay nothing. Many of their signs are forgotten within seconds. A company will burn through half a million dollars for a thirty-second television spot. If you land a good morning TV interview, you can reach the same number of viewers and actually *connect* with them—for free. If you create a contagious viral video and post it to YouTube, you can reach eight times more viewers than you would by appearing on *Larry King Live*. The possibilities are truly endless.

SECRET #58: DON'T TAKE ANYTHING PERSONALLY

If you're going to play with the big kids, you need to be prepared. Don't take anything personally. Getting national media attention is complex, and it rarely turns out *exactly* the way you expected it to, which is a good thing. This means the amount of attention you receive for your cause could be infinitely greater than you anticipated. It also means you will become a public target. Fifteen-year-olds will write mean things about you on their blogs; newspaper reporters will occasionally misquote you; that one radio interview may turn out kinda bad.

Can you handle this? It seems like a pretty small price to pay for receiving millions of dollars in "advertising" for free. Suck it up and **take nothing personally.** That's a major secret, and the sooner you learn it, the better. Writers and producers go for a good story; they aren't there just to make you look awesome. They don't care about making you famous either; that's just a byproduct. They care about a good story above all else. You're being *used* in a lot of respects. That's not a terrible thing—you get used all the time without your permission. Every time you log in to your email account, for instance, you're being used—you view a bunch of ads you didn't explicitly agree to view. You don't even think twice about it. It's the same thing with media attention. If you want to put an optimistic spin on it, you could say that your relationships with networks and

193 | ★

publications are actually *symbiotic.* You need them; they need you. A TV talk show can't exist without fascinating guests, and you can't prosper without people knowing about you.

You know that famous scene in the movie *Wall Street* where Gordon Gekko proclaims that "greed is good"? Well, I believe that fame is good. It's a force that will propel your business forward, get serious attention for your cause, and jump-start whatever else you're trying to accomplish in life. There are those in entertainment and some old-school media reporters who feel this is wrong. They would prefer if people like Julia Allison were confined to an island somewhere. This "old-school" train of thought is very simple: You do something well, and then you become famous for that. Or you don't.

Don't get me wrong; I like the idea of that—fame being eventually bestowed upon those who deserve it the most. However, we live in the real world. Take one quick glance at the tabloids, and you'll have plenty of evidence that fame is not a meritocracy. It's a free for all, a race to the top, an unpredictable commodity.

The Internet and other modern forms of communication forever altered how the system works. You don't do something well and then hope for fame to knock on your door. Many major Internet companies don't want you to buy anything from them. They just want you to stay on their site, viewing and clicking on ads in the process. Attention is the most coveted thing these days.

In the modern media climate, you become famous, and *then* you pursue specialized projects. Let's say you aspire to become a Broadway actor. You work hard, perfect your craft, and remain unnoticed. Meanwhile, some "no-talent" actor from a low-brow sitcom—or worse, a reality show—is picked as the lead for a new musical. The show's producers, at the end of the day, want to draw people in. They want a name on the billboards that people have heard of, for potential audiences to say, "Oh, I like him. I want to see that!" Talent is still important (if "stars" like Julia didn't give great interviews, they wouldn't last on-air), but it's not enough anymore. We only care about notoriety as a society now. I don't know if that's a good or bad thing, but I do know that it's a natural result of being bombarded with commercial messages. We're the most attention deficit-addled generation in history: If we haven't *already* seen you on YouTube, laughed at you on Jay Leno, or read about you online, chances are we won't be compelled to support your brand merely by your skill at whatever you're doing.

Some academics would have you believe that the creeping predominance of celebrity stories in the media is some kind of clever diversion. We talk about the fluff instead of the meaningful issues. This isn't what's going on. As I explained in the first chapter, the media is for profit. The simple truth is that more people will watch a segment about a celebrity meltdown than a PBS-style documentary about yet another inefficient aspect of government. And unless human nature drastically changes course in the next few years (I'm betting it won't!), celebrity culture will become an ever more important aspect of life. We like to be entertained. What's so wrong about that?! Fame is good.

SECRET #59: A LITTLE ZEN READING PROBABLY WON'T KILL YOU

A buzz whore's life is enhanced when he has a quiet inner mind, young grasshopper. No, but seriously, you should consider taking a meditation course or at least picking up a book of Zen koans at your local bookstore. A koan is a kind of riddle or poem that temporarily detaches your mind from all of the little concerns we spend so much of our time worrying about. I find it helpful to meditate for a few minutes before doing an interview, or to reflect on a koan I've recently read.

I recommend *Zen Flesh, Zen Bones*—it's an excellent collection of Zen koans, and it's in paperback, too. *The Power of Now* is also a great read. "Present moment awareness" will help you do on-air interviews without any unnecessary stress.

I like the contrast in my life between a stressful external environment (deadlines, interviews, flaky producers rescheduling on you) and a quiet inner environment. Confidence comes naturally to me, but patience does not. Zen koans and basic meditation will help you overcome impatience, which is helpful when you're first striking out and building buzz. It will also keep you focused on what's important: Getting massive attention for you or your cause. In other words, you'll learn over time not to fixate on the one bad review or interview. You'll focus on the 99 percent of your public life that is actually good.

SECRET #60: ALL PUBLICITY WAVES ARE TEMPORARY

Zen will also give you some perspective on imperma-
nence. Life is short, business cycles are short, and
publicity waves are often very short. You need to accept
this and let go. When a wave of buzz "dies," it's a good
thing, believe it or not. It frees you up to pursue a new
project, learn from your past experiences, and create
something ultimately even more powerful. If you keep
trying, it's only a matter of time before you stumble
upon the perfectly viral video or concept. It's such a
weird and amazing experience when you do finally hit
oil, so to speak. There isn't really a middle ground.
You're either starving for publicity or the phone is ringing off the hook with interview requests. As I've
mentioned earlier, make it a habit to read through the
social bookmarking sites like Del.icio.us and Digg. Get a
good, gut-level feel for what kind of idea is likely to go
viral. And then try it. The risks are often very low, and
the payoff is often very high.

**I think if you embrace the unpredictability of it
all, while at the same time trying your best to
predict which ideas will take off, you safeguard
your mental well-being.** A lot of who-gets-famous-
and-who-doesn't has nothing to do with us. It comes down
to producers liking an idea, bored Internet surfers forward-
ing a web page to their friends, being the "expert" in the
right place at the right time, and just sheer luck. We cannot
control all of these variables. That's why a laid-back and

Zen-minded buzz monger is a force to be reckoned with. You won't get discouraged when ideas fail to take off, and you won't become an obnoxious diva after you've had one or two major successes.

Maintain a lighthearted attitude, and enter new situations with as few expectations as possible. As I've said before, it's possible that the coverage you receive will greatly exceed your expectations, so why limit yourself? Expectations are a waste of time, particularly if you're scaring yourself about the consequences.

SECRET #61: EMBRACING CHAOS AND THE NEWS CYCLE

When you hit upon a great idea and your publicity campaign takes off, it will soon become unpredictable. Let go, and don't become overly controlling. If you attempt to completely "own" whatever happens, you are stifling it. The most powerful viral campaigns are, well, *viral.* A virus cannot be entirely predicted or contained. Just understand what's happening, and go with the flow. Let people add to the fire—make sure social bookmarking sites know about your new hit. Make sure every single person you know on Facebook knows your website address or the time you'll be on TV: Encourage them to tell others.

I think I've already said this enough, **but be okay with chaos.** Life is chaotic and unpredictable anyway, so you might as well learn to live with it! Plus, chaos sells—the media loves a degree of chaos.

★ 198

SECRET #62: THE PART OF THE BOOK WHERE I PLUG MY WEBSITE

If you want to contact me, visit www.shutterline.com. My contact info is posted over there, along with links to some of my existing projects. If you end up emailing me, put "Dirty Little Secrets" in the subject line so I know you're not spam or my long-lost friend from fifth grade or something crazy.

Epilogue

Epilogue

★
★ ★
★ ★
··

A POWERFUL PREDICTION

★

As I was working on this book, the Writer's Guild of America was on strike. TV shows and series were without writers to produce timely new material for fourteen weeks. It was a mess for everyone involved, brought about by a rising entertainment medium: the Internet. Studios are afraid because they have very little control over the distribution of their content: People are no longer just watching TV. They're using TiVo and watching their favorite shows whenever they want, they're fast-forwarding through commercials, they're downloading their favorites shows through BitTorrent file-sharing websites.

The writers in Hollywood wanted a piece of this new action. They wanted a percentage of the revenue coming in from new media—iTunes video downloads, advertising-supported video clips, and so forth. People are still watching shows, probably more than ever. They just aren't watching them in a controlled environment.

In a few years, it won't make sense for networks and big media companies to invest all of their resources in a few shows. Instead, it will make sense to fund tons of micro-shows on the Internet. Give each of the shows some marketing dollars and see what happens—let the people decide which shows are most popular and then ratchet up marketing and production resources for those shows. In this sense, the Internet becomes a valuable farming system for new content. This is already the case with blogs—if a story breaks on a small but respected weblog, it will likely then get mainstream media coverage if it has national significance.

It's no surprise that News Corp., one of the largest media conglomerates on Earth, snatched up MySpace. The site is a perfect platform for launching and testing new shows. In fact, the site recently launched MySpaceTV, where Web "episodes" are aired. These are essentially budding micro-shows.

Anyway, why should you care about all of this? Here's why: The barriers to entry into fame are the lowest they have *ever* been. In other words, if you create a MySpace profile and a few successful viral videos, you'll begin to attract a following. With the rise of social book-marking sites and feed-based social networks, your success can be amplified ten or a hundredfold literally overnight. At this point, the large media companies will pounce on you and find a way to profit from what they perceive as a marketable new commodity: You!

This was probably part of the reason why Google acquired YouTube. Of course, in reality, there's a flaw here. Not *everyone* on YouTube is a star. A lot of it is goofy crap that only gets a few hundred views. In fact, YouTube itself may not be the platform of choice for videos a couple years from now, but that's irrelevant. What matters is that building a core audience is easier than ever before. You can test a new idea with very little financial or time commitment. And if it hits, it hits *big*. I mentioned earlier in the book how ABC News swooped in and snatched up Amanda Congdon as her online popularity skyrocketed. I've also mentioned how Dane Cook used the Internet to catapult himself to fame. In the future, this will be the norm, not the exception. The United States is rapidly becoming a nation of Tila Tequilas where the only currency that matters is how many people know you.

In many ways, my "farming system" prediction is already how conventional book publishing works. Publishers don't just acquire a few titles a year. They acquire a bunch, give each of them *some* marketing resources, and then wait and see which ones take off. Once a title is showing strong growth, then the publisher ratchets up the marketing push. In other words, it's a content gamble. Publishers can *predict* which titles will be hits (usually ones written by big-name authors do well, obviously), but they can't be 100 percent certain until the sales numbers start to roll in.

The same thing will occur with television shows. A network may fund a hundred new online shows per year and watch to see which ones get a disproportionate number of viewers. Even if only 3 percent of the micro-shows end up doing well, that means the network has found three new shows with *huge* potential. That more than covers the bandwidth and production costs for the rest of the lower-performing shows.

If you were smart (if I were smart!), we would have started building our online platforms at least seven years ago. Don't be hard on yourself, though. Up until recently, the Internet has been largely static. This shift toward dynamically created content is fairly new, and the interest from big media in user-created content is newer still.

Besides, you don't need to have seven or eight years of presence to create an online hit. By the very nature of *viral* content, you can create something and have it become a worldwide sensation within hours. Mediocre buzz whores only collect contacts and build their newsletters. Yes, it's important to build up your fan base; I can't disagree with that. But the really crucial thing is to create something snappy, new, and weird that people will *want* to tell their friends about. At the end of the day, you can't force people to make you famous. It needs to be dynamic. A successful viral video or concept will take *you* along for the ride and not the other way around. At a certain point, it takes on a life of its own. You can't really control it at this point; you can only step back and observe as things take off. This is part of the reason why I don't think it's insane to use an Eastern point of view (present moment awareness, Zen practice, etc.) to help pinpoint the next mega-viral trend. Word of mouth is chaotic and infinitely more powerful than we expect it to be.

When I talk to slightly older people about this shift in the avenues toward fame, I sometimes use the metaphor of a skipping stone. It's aptly Zen and actually describes the viral process well. You pick up a stone and throw it into a pond. It goes *kerplunk* and promptly sinks to the bottom. That's how most online content ends up: You put it out there, a few people check it out, and then it fades into obscurity. It sinks. But, let's say you scour the shoreline for a flat, relatively thin pebble and toss it into the pond at just the right angle. What happens seems magical. The stone skips off the surface, bounces off the surface a second time, and a third time, maybe even a fourth time. It takes off.

Of course, on the Internet, if something bounces a few times, that means it can bounce a few million times. Once something is popular with a core group of people, it can quickly become popular with an infinitely large group of people. Social networks may not *actually* bring people any closer together in terms of their interpersonal relationships; if anything, social networks alienate people. They make interactions *less* personal. What they really do best is make it infinitely easy to share content that is perceived as valuable, different, or new.

A New American Tradition

Buzz whoring is perhaps the last living piece of the American Dream. People emerge into the national consciousness every single day using unconventional means. Fifty years ago, you weren't famous unless a major Hollywood studio said you were. Today, that's just about irrelevant. Not on *American Idol?* Don't have famous parents? No marketable talents? It's no excuse: Set up a blog and get a feel for the sort of transient online firestorms making folks famous today.

It's part of the American Dream, and by extension it brings you closer to God. OK, I'm totally kidding. But the buzz whore enjoys a position that few others in society can experience. It's the twenty-first century court jester, political commentator, and philosopher-king all rolled into one.

Thanks to the Internet, multinational media conglomerates too lazy to create their own content, and to an apparent ADD pandemic, it is now honestly possible to become a household name with a four-minute YouTube video. This level of word-of-mouth power is still quite new. Even ten years ago, a book like *The Dirty Little Secrets of Buzz* would have been mere fantasy.

Culture and media have converged in a wonderfully weird way. People *love* to tell others about the latest Chris Crocker type—*someone* forwarded his video to you, after all. Someone found him irresistible, if a little demented. The television networks and the radio programs want to feel relevant. "Look what we found!" they excitedly tell viewers each evening. For this reason, many shows will latch onto something right as it is becoming mainstream. They'll give your cause the extra boost needed to make it over the edge.

Ours is a world where only newness and novelty matter. You don't need connections; you only need temporary relevance. You don't need billboards or megaphones, just an account at Del.icio.us or StumbleUpon. Even billionaires and large corporations are vulnerable to the new buzz—they want to profit from it, but they don't want to get burned by it. Kids in their grandparents' basements and garage bands out in the middle of nowhere are the new marketing execs. Every friend listed on your MySpace page is potentially your most loyal promoter. It's luck, chaos, and gut instinct that determines who will be talked about at the proverbial water cooler next Monday.

These are exciting times. A little amoral and vacuous? Sure, maybe. But I'm not complaining. This isn't going away; it's just going to get bigger and bigger. There's no other alternative. So embrace it, stay Zen so you don't kill yourself when things heat up, and constantly think in terms of whether something has viral potential or not.

It isn't always the smartest or the best idea that is heard. It's the idea that people forward to their friends, it's the video of that dude getting Tasered, it's a picture of Jack Nicholson looking sloppy at the beach. People want some familiarity, but not too much. What everyone really wants is absurd novelty, and if you can find a way to package your cause in such a way, you'll be set. Good luck.

207 ★

APPENDIX

Additional Resources

Here are some additional websites, services, and books worth checking out; every buzz whore should be aware of these.

SERVICES

http://www.aweber.com

AWeber is hands-down the best professional newsletter management system out there. I use them to run my newsletters and the deliverability rate is generally quite high (above 99 percent).

http://www.massmediadistribution.com

MMD Newswire is a great way to hit lots of news desks with a killer hook or press release. Only use this service if you have a truly perfect hook, however, as it does cost quite a bit.

http://www.prweb.com

PRWeb is an affordable press release service with real-time online statistics showing how many journalists have read or printed out your release. The service is good because it provides valuable search-engine positioning for releases you post there. PRWeb presumably has a high PageRank and can help attract targeted visitors from search engines such as Google.

http://www.ereleases.com

This is a pricey service, but they do great work, and a release on eReleases is also picked up by PR Newswire, which has significant reach. This company also offers professional release writing and editing.

WEBSITES

http://www.twitter.com

Online personal update system: If you want to build a "bond" with readers on your site or blog, this is an interesting way to keep people involved. You can login from any Internet connection or your mobile phone and post exactly what you're doing right now ("editing my book at the beach!")—the service will automatically post the update to your website and broadcast it to friends.

http://www.stumbleupon.com

Get a StumbleUpon account, and start using it to promote your latest causes and viral videos. Use the networking features of SU to build up a circle of "friends"—some people believe this increases your power on the network, and thus the number of visitors you can direct to a site you recommend. Plus, it's kind of fun!

http://www.ebaumsworld.com

Many of the videos on eBaum's World are profoundly dumb. With that said, it's a site where individual videos profit tremendously from viral, word-of-mouth buzz, so it's worth checking out purely as a case study. Why do certain videos take off while others remain relatively unknown?

http://www.tribe.net

Tribe is a localized social networking site; good way to seed new causes and viral concepts within a certain area or city.

http://www.wikipedia.org

Just paying homage to Wikipedia here. Although teachers and college professors may rail against the free-for-all, anonymously edited encyclopedia, it remains one of the most important resources on the Web. It's a great starting point for researching anything—and contrary to common belief, many of the facts on there *can* be easily verified (just check the original sources at the bottom of each page).

http://www.shutterline.com

Of course you'll want to visit my site for the latest buzz tips and to find out about upcoming appearances. My email address is also posted over there should you have any questions not covered in the book or need me to take a look at your press release.

BOOKS

The Power of Now by **Eckhart Tolle**

Great present-moment-awareness book, probably the best one out there. An "in-the-moment" worldview is helpful when building a buzz campaign, especially during challenging interviews.

The Definitive Book of Body Language by **Barbara and Allan Pease**

Aside from being an excellent read, this book is how I first learned about "power words" such as easy, free, discover, and so forth. Shortly after reading the book, I had the idea of implementing these words in on-air interviews and in online buzz marketing materials. You can also use basic body language techniques to create rapport with television hosts and viewers. It's totally sneaky but a great idea!

213 ★

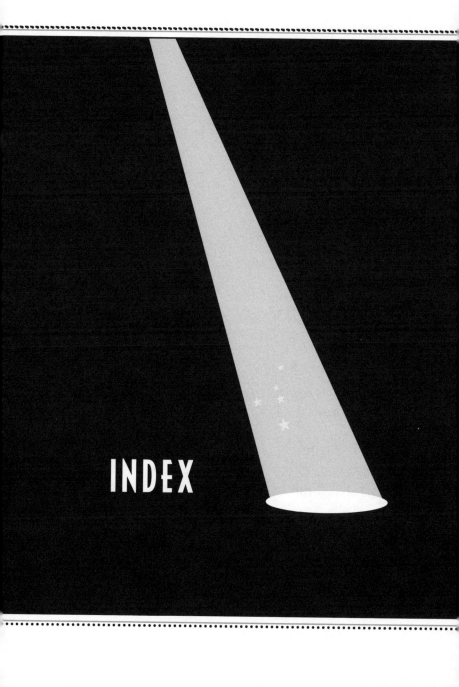

INDEX

About the Author

 David Seaman is a full-time writer, blogger, and media personality. Seaman is the founder of Shutterline Interactive, a vehicle for rapidly deploying new publicity stunts. He has appeared on numerous TV and radio programs, including *CNN Headline News*, *CBS Radio News*, and FOX's *The Morning Show*, and has been quoted in countless publications all over the world.